Three Medieval Latin Liturgical Dramas:

The Three Students,

The Play of Daniel

and

Hildegard of Bingen's

The Play of the Virtues

An Intermediate Latin Reader

C. T. HADAVAS

Three Medieval Latin Liturgical Dramas: *The Three Students*, *The Play of Daniel* and Hildegard of Bingen's *The Play of the Virtues*
An Intermediate Latin Reader
Latin text with vocabulary and commentary

First Edition
(Revised March 2014)

The Latin texts are modified versions of those in Dronke 1994. Changes, designed to make the texts more accessible and readable to students, include the spelling of certain words and the simplification of the colometry.

ISBN-13: 978-1491013526
ISBN-10: 1491013524

Published by C. T. Hadavas

Cover Design: C. T. Hadavas
Cover Image: Detail from Rembrandt's "Belshazzar's Feast" (1635; National Gallery, London), a scene dramatically represented by lines 46a-48 of the second play in this edition, the *Danielis Ludus* ("The Play of Daniel").

Font: Times

hadavasc@beloit.edu

Table of Contents

Preface

This edition makes available to students three dramatic works of Medieval Latin literature. The earliest of these, the eleventh-century *Tres Clerici* ("The Three Students"), recounts one of the miracles of that most popular of medieval saints, Nicholas. This drama's economical construction and refined use of a simple metrical unit exemplify how a playwright can convey much in few words.

The other two plays included in this collection are the outstanding examples of Latin liturgical drama composed in the twelfth century. The *Danielis Ludus* ("The Play of Daniel"), written in the cathedral school of Beauvais, adapts material from the Bible to relate the meaning of a story from the ancient past – the Hebrew prophet Daniel's interactions with two foreign rulers, Belshazzar and Darius – to contemporary issues. This play's rhetorical sophistication, metrical variety, and musical invention are unsurpassed in the dramatic works from this period.

Hildegard of Bingen's *Ordo Virtutum* ("The Play of the Virtues") has the distinction of being the only play in this group whose author is not anonymous. Hildegard left behind more than just a name, however, for her impressive literary, scientific, theological, and musical oeuvre rivals those of her more traditionally educated male peers in quality and surpasses them in diversity. In addition, Hildegard's female-centered play, whose verses are rich with symbolism, fuses together liturgical drama and theological allegory in an innovative manner that anticipates the new genre of morality plays written in the vernacular languages two centuries later.

A commentator is, to a great extent, a compiler and arranger of other scholars' ideas. The most important ideas in the field of Medieval Latin liturgical drama in the last half century have been those of Peter Dronke, Professor (and now, in his retirement, an Emeritus Fellow) of Medieval Latin Literature at the University of Cambridge. Dronke's provocative and enlightening studies first sparked my interest in these plays many years ago. References to his research are scattered liberally throughout my notes. Indeed, it is a rare page in this commentary that is not touched, either directly or indirectly, by his academic spirit.

I would like to thank my colleague, Art Robson, Emeritus Professor of Classics at Beloit College, for a critical reading of an earlier draft of this edition. Art's helpful suggestions forced me to rethink and clarify many of my ideas, and to jettison others in which I could not meet his exacting standards. The text before you is leaner – and better – because of Art's assistance.

C. T. Hadavas
Beloit, Wisconsin
July 2013

Introduction

1 Medieval Drama

(*i*) Drama in the Early Middle Ages

After the fall of the Roman Empire in the fifth century CE, the large outdoor theaters of Europe, Asia Minor, and North Africa began to decay. Even before this physical deterioration, however, Christian apologists and Church fathers such as Tertullian (*c.* 160-220) and Augustine (354-430) had vehemently attacked the non-Christian popular theater (which included gladiatorial shows, games, and spectacles as well as traditional plays) as the Devil's instrument.[1] Their sermons and writings, which urged Christians to avoid such entertainments with their pagan associations and often graphic displays of violence and bloodshed, were quite successful: the Olympic Games were closed down after more than one thousand years in existence, gladiatorial shows were prohibited, and comedies and tragedies were banished from the stage. Yet the dramatic instinct managed to survive into the Middle Ages, though in a rather transformed state.

Despite the fact that there are almost no surviving texts from the period *c.* 450-950, there is much evidence that a lively and varied dramatic activity continued throughout Europe. The most important sources are (ironically) the numerous prohibitions issued by the Church, as well as individual letters of clergy who condemned various types of theatrical performances. This evidence paints a picture of travelling players, known as *mimi*, *ludatores*, *ioculatores* or *histriones*, who provided dramatic entertainment as they toured villages, towns, courts, and, surprisingly, monasteries. The range of these early performers was quite wide, and included storytelling, magic tricks, juggling, ventriloquism, and dancing.

Sometime in the tenth century the monastic schools began to produce imitations of the dramatic works of classical authors they had copied and kept in their libraries, especially those of the comic playwright Terence (*c.* 190-159 BCE), as exercises in grammar and rhetoric as well as for religious expression. The first surviving plays from this period are those of Hrotsvitha of Gandersheim, who revived text-based drama in the mid-tenth century with a series of theatrical works on Christian themes. Her most famous play, *Dulcitius*, is a dramatization of the martyrdom of three sisters who lived during the persecution of Diocletian (*c.* 300 CE), the last to be waged against the Christians. It is almost certain, however, that Hrotsvitha's plays were never meant to be staged.[2]

---

[1] Paterno 1989, 7-24 gives a brief overview of twelve of the most significant early church fathers and their opinions on the pagan theater.

[2] Sticca 1985 provides a stimulating essay on the nature of Hrotsvitha's literary dramas.

(*ii*) Religious and Secular Drama in the High and Late Middle Ages

Scholars continue to debate the exact origins of liturgical drama, a genre that included the first documented theatrical texts that were actually performed in the Middle Ages. It seems clear, however, that Hrotsvitha's works played, at best, only a sporadic and subsidiary role in the development of later performance drama.[3] What one can say unreservedly about liturgical drama is that throughout its early history (1050-1200) it retained an intimate connection to the Church linguistically, physically, and spiritually. This is not at all surprising, since this particular genre probably evolved in some way from liturgical offices developed during the tenth and eleventh centuries to enhance calendar festivals, especially those during Christmas and Easter. And it is no accident that this type of drama was developed for this purpose, since its appearance in the eleventh century coexisted with, and was probably a response to, the economic vibrancy that was especially felt at this time in the religious institutions of the Church. The splendid new cathedrals that were built, the costly vestments employed by clergy, and the protracted religious celebrations and magnificent processions coupled with a heightened sense of the significance of cult were all important factors in the creation and promotion of Church-based theatrical works. These elements came to a head in the twelfth century, a period which saw the greatest development of Latin liturgical drama, including the two very different works presented in this collection: the *Danielis Ludus* from Beauvais and Hildegard of Bingen's *Ordo Virtutum*.

Religious dramas of this period, unlike their secular counterparts, were almost exclusively written and sung in Latin (especially the plays that date from the eleventh to thirteenth centuries) or in a mixture of Latin and the vernacular (most are from the twelfth century, such as the *Danielis Ludus*). There also exist later religious plays (from 1375) written entirely in the vernacular languages of Europe (primarily English, German, French, Spanish, and Italian). These differed from the Latin liturgical dramas in that they often contained broadly comic scenes and buffoonish characters (devils, villains, etc.) that were enormously popular with the masses. The two types of religious drama also differed in terms of performers and locations. In the Latin liturgical plays the actors were at first drawn from the members of the clergy or the choirboys, and later included students and scholars of the cathedral schools. These dramas were exclusively staged in churches and cathedrals.[4] Acting in the vernacular dramas, however, was a community event in which both clergy and townspeople participated on fixed stages that were set up not only in churches, but also along the outside of churches, in courtyards, or in town squares.

The one similarity shared by both Latin and vernacular religious plays was that they took their plots from the same narrative sources. The majority of the these plays retell famous stories from the Bible (e.g., Creation, Noah and the Ark, Daniel in the Lions' Den, etc.),

---

[3] See Dronke 1994, xix-xx for a possible connection between Hrotsvithas' works and the *Tres Clerici*.

[4] Several studies examine how the church architecture of the period may have been exploited by the actors in these productions. For the *Ordo Virtutum*, see Davidson 1992; for the *Danielis Ludus*, see Ogden 1996b.

with a special focus on the life of Christ. These dramas are sometimes called by modern scholars mystery plays. Other liturgical dramas that present an account (in most cases largely fictitious) of the life, miracles, or martyrdom of a saint or other exemplary figure are called miracle or saints plays. The *Tres Clerici* ("The Three Students") in this edition is an example of one such play depicting a miracle performed by St. Nicholas.

Debate also continues over the origins in the late thirteenth century of secular drama, a genre that consisted of plays performed in the vernacular languages of Europe (often in regional dialects). Except for the occasional song, the texts of these dramas were spoken, not sung, and performed by both amateurs and professionals[5] on fixed stages, temporarily erected either indoors or outdoors. The most popular secular dramas were the morality plays, which used allegorical characters and situations in which actors personified a vice, virtue or some other abstract concept. These plays flourished from the fourteenth to the early sixteenth centuries (a famous example being the English drama *Everyman*, written *c.* 1500). Morality plays had invented plots (a rarity in this period), and were more explicitly pedagogical and ethical in their orientation than other theatrical works.

One rather anomalous drama that may be classified under this genre is Hildegard of Bingen's twelfth-century *Ordo Virtutum* ("The Play of the Virtues"). From a general typological perspective – the plot, revolving around the fate of a soul, is enacted by a cast of abstract personifications – Hildegard's *Ordo* is a morality play. But unlike the later morality plays, which it precedes by two centuries, the *Ordo* was sung to a Latin text and performed in an abbey. Such formal aspects as these, along with its elevated tone and sophisticated use of biblical allusion, relate it more closely to the liturgical dramas produced in the twelfth century.[6]

2 Medieval Latin

Medieval Latin is a catchall phrase that describes the four types (and various combinations of these four types) of Latin employed in Western Europe during the Middle Ages: Classical Latin, Late Latin, Ecclesiastical Latin, and Popular (or Vulgar) Latin.

Classical Latin existrd only as a literary language preserved in the classics of Roman literature of the late Republic and early Empire (c. 100 BCE-150 CE). Such authors as Cicero, Sallust, Virgil, Ovid, and Suetonius became the school texts by which students throughout the Middle Ages learned a variety of sophisticated literary styles against which their own prose and verse would be measured.

Late Latin describes the evolution of the literary language in the period following the early Empire up to the early Middle Ages (*c.* 150-550 CE). Late Latin includes more colloquial elements than Classical Latin and borrows more heavily from Classical Greek.

---

[5] By 1350 there was enough demand for performers that permanent troupes were established.

[6] For a comparison of the *Ordo Virtutum* to the later English morality plays, see Potter 1992.

As the empire dissolved into various semiautonomous regions, the Latin language followed course, and at the beginning of the Middle Ages (c. 450 CE) one can already observe embryonic aspects of the various vernaculars (e.g., Spanish, French, Italian) emerging from the mother tongue.

Ecclesiastical Latin is principally the creation of the early western Church apologists and fathers, preeminently Tertullian (*c*. 160-220), Ambrose (*c*. 339-97), Jerome (*c*. 340-420), and Augustine (354-430). Although educated in Classical Latin, these men sought to express themselves in a language that blended their classical training with that of the Latin translations of the Bible and the popular Latin of the common people. The result was a series of Christian classical works that were as highly esteemed in the Middle Ages as those of earlier pagan authors. By far the most influential of all these Christian works for the later Middle Ages was Jerome's translation of the Bible, known as the Vulgate, which eventually superseded earlier translations of the scriptures into Latin.[7]

Unlike the three previous categories of literary Latin, Popular Latin was the conversational language of daily life used throughout the history of the Latin language as a spoken tongue. Elements of this colloquial Latin can be found in authors as diverse in time as Plautus (*c*. 254-184 BCE) and Petronius (c. 60 CE). But Popular Latin existed long before Plautus and continued for many centuries after Petronius until in the end linguistic evolution and regional isolation led to the creation of the vernacular languages of Italian, Spanish, Portuguese, Catalan, French, and Romanian, along with their numerous regional dialects. The main characteristics of Popular Latin in the medieval period, especially when viewed from the perspective of Classical Latin, are a fondness for the diminutive, a preference for longer words and elaborate compounds over simpler constructions, and an expressive use of slang words and phrases.

Medieval Latin can, depending on the author's geography, time, level of education, and desired audience, contain one or more elements of Classical, Late, Ecclesiastical, and Popular Latin. It has no separate linguistic existence apart from its texts and varies more according to the educational level of a particular writer than it does geographically or chronologically. It is Latin that was learned principally by monks, nuns, and clergy from late antique grammars and daily exposure to the Bible and the liturgy. The variations in spelling that occur in medieval writers are due primarily to pronunciation changes that developed over time and in different regions. Occasional errors in morphology are most likely the result of the illiteracy of many of the writers. The syntax of Medieval Latin texts may be influenced by other languages (especially the writer's native tongue), while the vocabulary is greatly expanded to meet the needs of new social, political, intellectual, and religious environments. Medieval Latin came to an end during the Italian

[7] These older translations are collectively called by scholars the Vetus Latina ("Old Latin"). They held the field for several centuries, despite the fact that Jerome's version was translated from the best texts available to him in the original languages (the Vetus Latina were translations of the Greek version of the Old Testament known as the Septuagint). This is not at all surprising, since the tastes of religious believers are notoriously conservative in this matter – witness the continuing popularity of the King James translation of the Bible after four hundred years. By the ninth century, however, the Vulgate had become the version of the Bible used most commonly in medieval Europe.

Renaissance (*c.* 1350-1550) when it was replaced by scholars with what is now called Neo-Latin, an attempt to reproduce Ciceronian Classical Latin.[8]

****

In the notes all non-Classical Latin words have been glossed. In addition, Classical Latin (CL) words that have undergone spelling changes are glossed in their original Classical Latin form (e.g., **hec** = CL *haec*). When words of this type occur a second time within a text they are marked with an asterisk, a third time with two asterisks, and subsequently they no longer appear in the commentary.

---

[8] Perhaps the best introduction to Medieval Latin orthography, morphology, syntax, and grammar is Elliot 1997, which manages within its fifty-one pages to provide clear explanations for most of the unusual features that students who learned Classical Latin will encounter in their reading of Medieval Latin texts.

Timeline Of Medieval Civilization & Drama

500-900 Early Middle Ages

- Western Europe is primarily an oral society (the Church has an almost complete monopoly on literacy)
- Traveling storytellers, mimes, jugglers, magicians, singers, etc.

900-1050 Early Medieval Civilization

- Feudal system established
- Monasteries no longer simply act as preservers of learning but begin to play a more proactive role in education
- Plays by Hrosvitha of Gandersheim (*c*. 935-973)

1050-1300 High Middle Ages

- Towns increase in population as industry and trade redevelop
- Gothic architecture (*c*. 1150-1500)
- Crusades (1095-1272)
- Reemergence of the written word in all areas of society
- Establishment of cathedral schools (some of which become universities)
- Theatrical performances in churches (e.g., *Tres Clerici*, *Danielis Ludus*, Hildegard of Bingen's *Ordo Virtutum*)

1300-1500 Late Medieval Civilization

- Continued growth of towns and universities
- Church begins to share its position of authority with other institutions
- Trend toward secularism in drama accelerates

Abbreviations

abl.(ative)
abl.(ative) abs.(olute)
acc.(usative)
adj.(ective)
adv.(erb)
c. circa
cf. compare (Latin *confer*)
ch.(apter)
CL Classical Latin
d.(ied)
dat.(ive)
dep.(opent)
EL Ecclesiastical Latin
fem.(inine)
ff. following
fut.(ure)
gen.(itive)
H.(ildegard)
imper.(ative)
impf. (imperfect)
indecl.(inable)
indic.(ative)
inf.(initive)
LL Late Latin
masc.(uline)
ML Medieval Latin
neut.(er)
n.(ote)
nom.(inative)
OF Old French
p./pp. page(s)
part.(iciple)
pf. (perfect)
pl.(ural)
plupf. pluperfect
pres.(ent)
sing.(ular)
subj.(unctive)
v./vv. verse(s)
< = "from"

Tres Clerici

("The Three Students")

c. 1050-1100

"Nicholas the Bishop." ***Nuremberg Chronicle*****, fol. CXXXIIv.**

Introduction

1 Saint Nicholas

Saint Nicholas was the patron of scholars and the only non-biblical saint to feature in Medieval Latin plays. Nearly everything known concerning this saint is derived from later tradition. Born at Patara in the Roman province of Lycia (on the southwest coast of modern day Turkey) *c.* 270 CE, the only son of wealthy parents, he was imprisoned for his faith under the Roman emperor Diocletian (ruled from 284-305; died *c.* 312). Eventually freed after the accession of the first Roman Christian emperor, Constantine (313), he later became Bishop of Myra, a town also in Lycia. He died on December 6 (still his feast day[9]) between 345 and 352.[10]

The cult of Saint Nicholas was immensely popular in the Middle Ages, first in the eastern (Orthodox), and then later in the western (Catholic) Church.[11] Dronke (1994, 52) notes that, "the apogee of his cult in the West comes in the twelfth century, soon after the dramatic "translation" – i.e. theft – of his supposed bones from Myra in 1087, by sailors who brought them westward to Bari," a city of southeast Italy on the Adriatic Sea.

Since then his popularity in the West has (excuse the pun) snowballed. Indeed, his most recent reincarnation, via a nineteenth-century poem ("Twas the Night Before Christmas") by the American Classicist Clement C. Moore – with later illustrations by Thomas Nast – and the large-scale early twentieth-century advertising campaign of the Coca-Cola company (which shows no sign of letting up)[12], Santa Claus[13] has now begun to supplant the figure for whom Christians first celebrated Christmas as the symbol and meaning of this most popular holiday in the West.[14]

---

[9] Incidentally, Nicholas' feast day was the occasion of merrymaking and (sometimes) clerical rowdiness in the Middle Ages.

[10] I am indebted for much of the biographical information in this paragraph to Dronke 1994, 52.

[11] By the end of the fifteenth century, St. Nicholas was the third most beloved religious figure in Christendom, after Jesus and Mary. There were by this time more than two thousand chapels and monasteries in Europe named after him.

[12] Clement C. Moore captured the public's imagination with this poem that he wrote for his children and which he published anonymously on December 23, 1823 in New York's *Sentinel*. Thomas Nast, a nineteenth-century American cartoonist and political satirist, later illustrated the story, depicting St. Nicholas in his now familiar red suit and hat, black boots and belt, white gloves, and flowing white beard (Nast's pipe has largely disappeared, in light of the relatively recent view on the dangers of smoking). Nast, however, depicted him as a small, gnome-like creature. It was the advertisers at Coca-Cola who made him into a full-size man, replete with a bottle of Coke in one hand and a broad smile on his rosy-cheeked face.

[13] The name Santa Claus is derived from the Dutch form of his name, *Sinta Klass*, which, in turn, comes from the Latin *Sancta Nicolaus*, itself a translation (*Sancta* < Ἅγιος [Hagios; "Saint"]) and transliteration (*Nicolaus* < Νικόλαος) of the Greek Ἅγιος Νικόλαος). It was the Dutch in their colony of New Amsterdam, now known as New York, who brought the tradition of St. Nicholas to America.

[14] In the West, Nicholas' activities have been moved from his traditional holy day, December 6, when he was believed to visit children with gifts, in preparation for the gift of the Christ child at Christmas, to December 25 itself. Other ironies abound in the Nicholas tradition. For example, Lycia, with its warm Mediterranean climate, rarely gets snow (and then, only on the peaks of its eastern mountains).

2 Date of Composition and Sources

The author of the *Tres Clerici* is unknown. Based on internal evidence (especially the writer's use of meter and his peculiar spellings), Dronke (1994, 60-1) conjectures that he was most likely a scholar of French origin who composed his work sometime in the second half of the eleventh century, a time that would coincide with the removal of Nicholas' relics from Myra to Bari. Since this play is the earliest surviving account of this particular miracle performed by St. Nicholas, it seems likely that the playwright based his story on one of the many oral legends that had been circulating publicly for centuries around this saint and not on some lost written account. Indeed, non-biblical texts in general were quite scarce before the eleventh century. Our anonymous author's play thus reveals him to be one of the pioneers of the revolution from oral transmission to the written word that marks this period in western civilization.[15]

3 Meter

Unlike Classical Latin verse, which is quantitative (i.e., syllabic length is its patterning agent), Medieval Latin verse can be either quantitative or accentual (i.e., a series of stressed and unstressed syllables is the patterning agent).[16] The latter is used in the *Tres Clerici*.

The metrical unit employed in the *Tres Clerici* is the quatrain, a four-verse stanza that concludes with a four-syllable line. The first four verses (which also have two-syllable end rhyme) of each stanza consist of lines that follow the metrical pattern of four syllables (usually two trochees) – word break – six syllables (usually two dactyls). Verse 3, for example, scans as follows: *cógit férre pénas exílii*.[17]

The most important accent is that of the third-last syllable of the second half of the verse (known as the proparoxytone; in v. 3 the proparoxtyonic stress falls on the second syllable of *exílii*). This is the strongest stress felt in the line and the one that holds invariably for all verses of this length in the play.

---

[15] For a brief discussion of this literary revolution, see pp. 31-32 (**1 Cathedral Schools** and **2 *Danielis Ludus*** (*i*) A School Text) below.

[16] This is the type of verse that is most often used in English poetry (the other type being free verse).

[17] This metrical pattern is the most common in the play. Variations on this pattern, however, also occur. Verse 1, for example, scans as follows: *Hóspes cáre trés súmus sótii*. This pattern is also found in vv. 2, 7, 11, 19, 34, 44, 51, 54, and 58. Even in v. 1, however, the stronger emphasis on *tres* and the corresponding weaker emphasis on the first syllable of *sumus* allow the phrase *tres sumus* to be read as a dactyl (i.e., *trés sumus*). Still other variations include v. 26 (*cóniux, sí fíeret*), though here too the phrase can be scanned as a dactyl (as is the case with verses similar to 26, such as vv. 56 and 61). This is also the case with verses that begin with four-syllable words, such as v. 2, where the word *litterarum* can be scanned either as two unaccented syllables followed by a trochee (i.e., *litterárum*) or the first half of the word is a (weakly) felt trochee (whose stress mark I note by a raised caret: i.e., *lîtterárum*). This is also true of such concluding fifth-verse examples as *hospitare* (v. 5) and *habeamus* (v. 25). There remain, however, a substantial number of verses whose meter does not fit any of these patterns. The most important of these are pointed out in the commentary. For an accessible and sensitive exploration of the flexibility of accentual meter, see Pinsky 1998.

The fifth verse of each stanza consists of four syllables, usually both trochees.[18] The only verses that stand outside of these rules are those spoken by the Choir (which are irregular, since they follow liturgical choral meters) and the final verse of the play that is spoken by an Angel, which is four syllables + eight syllables (but still keeping the proparoxytonic stress at the end).

Although the *Tres Clerici* was originally sung, its musical score does not survive.

[18] Exceptions are vv. 30 (*infámia*), 60 (*diútius*) and 65 (*pér córpora*).

Tres Clerici

Primus clericus:

Hospes care, tres sumus sotii
litterarum quos causa studii
cogit ferre penas exilii—
nos sub tui tectis hospitii
        hospitare!   5

Secundus:

Fessi sumus longo itinere:
tempus esset iam nos quiesere.
Nobis velis amoris federe
hospitium noctu concedere
        quo egemus.   10

Speech 1: First Student (1-5)

The first student informs us that he and his friends are wandering scholars enduring "exile" for the sake of their education.[19] Note the extensive (13x) (ingratiating?) use of the sibilant "s" throughout his speech, which mingles at the end in vv. 4 and 5 with the harsher dental "t". Note too the repetition of the root "hosp" in the first and last two words of the stanza: "hospitality" is one of the key themes of this play and the one which – ironically – the *hospes* will soon reveal that he conspicuously lacks.

1 sotii = CL *socii* < *socius*, *-i*: "friend."
2 litterarum quos causa studii = *quos causa studii litterarum.*
3 penas = CL *poenas* < *poena*, *-ae*: "punishment," "pain."
4 sub tui tectis hospitii = *sub tectis hospitii tui.* **hospitii** < *hospitium*, *-i*: "inn," "lodging."
5 hospitare: inf. as imper. (a common usage in ML and modeled on the Greek mediated through the use of EL).

Speech 2: Second Student (6-10)

Whereas the first student explained why they are abroad, the second student adds the important information that they are exhausted and in need of rest before making his passionate appeal to the innkeeper to allow them to stay the night. Note the continued use of "s" (12x) in this stanza.

6 Fessi < *fessus*, *-a*, *-um*: "tired," "exhausted."
7 quiesere = CL *quiescere.*
8-9 Nobis . . . egemus = *federe amoris velis concedere nobis hospitium quo egemus noctu.*
8 velis (pres. subj.) < *volo*, *velle*: "to be willing." **federe** = CL *foedere* < *foedus*, *-eris*: "bond." **noctu:** (adv.) "at night."

---

[19] In the Middle Ages education (called the *artes*) consisted of two divisions of knowledge: (1) the *quadrivium*, i.e., arithmetic, geometry, astronomy, and music; (2) the *trivium*, i.e., logic, grammar, and rhetoric. Together they made up the "seven liberal arts" that were regarded as constituting a necessary course of study for an educated person. Hollister (1982, 291) adds that, "on the successful completion of the liberal arts curriculum, the student could apply for a license to teach, but might also wish to continue his studies by specializing in medicine, theology, or civil or canon law." Like many young people in the eleventh century, the three students of this play left their homes or native countries (usually England, France, and Italy) and took to the road in pursuit of some famous teacher whose reputation had reached their land.

Tertius:

Sommo mane cras, hospes, ibimus:
non de tuo vivere querimus,
quia victum nobiscum gerimus—
hospitium tantum deposimus,
causa Dei. 15

Respondeat hospes:

Cum vos ita fessos conspitiam,
propter summam Dei clementiam
vos hic intus noctu sucipiam—
vobis ignem cum lecto fatiam.
Ite sessum. 20

Uxor, audi meum consilium:
isti scensum gerunt eximium—
inpendamus eis exitium,
ut eorum tesauri pretium
habeamus! 25

Speech 3: Third Student (11-15)

Whereas all three students ask the innkeeper for a night's lodging, it is the third, in an attempt to reassure him that they will not be any trouble since they have with them their own provisions, who unknowingly discloses that he and his friends are not poor, starving vagrants. His speech contains similar alliteration (e.g., "s" 12x) to and verbal reflections (*hospes*, *hospitium*) of those made by his two friends. But building on the second student's "bond of love" appeal, he also adds the element of Christian charity (*causa Dei*) – an idea that will become central at the conclusion of the play.

11 Sommo mane = CL *Summo mane* (i.e., "At earliest dawn"). **ibimus** < *eo*, *-ire*: "to go."

12 tuo: "your own <food>." **Querimus** = CL *Quaerimus* < *quaero*, *-ere*: "to ask (for)," "seek to obtain."

14 deposimus = CL *deposcimus* < *deposco*, *-ere*: "to request urgently," "beg," "beseech."

Speech 4: Innkeeper (16-25)

In the first stanza the innkeeper replies to the students with extravagant geniality (note the triple repetition of *vos*) and generosity. Especially noteworthy are his verbal echoes of the students' ideas (e.g., *fessos*, *Dei*) and the repetition of "s" (9x). After the students have gone to sleep, the innkeeper attempts to enlist his wife in a nefarious plan. The good qualities he expressed in his previous speech are now shown to have been merely a façade as he is revealed to be a cold-blooded killer obsessed with money (*scensum . . . eximium*; *tesauri pretium*). The labial-nasal "m", "am" and "um" sounds in both stanzas are particularly prominent.

16 conspitiam = CL *conspiciam* (pres. subj.) < *conspicio*, *-ere*: "to see."

18 sucipiam = CL *suscipiam* (fut.) < *suscipio*, *-ere*: "to receive," "welcome."

19 fatiam = CL *faciam*.

20 Ite sessum: "Come sit down," "Come rest."

22 scensum = CL *censum* < *census*, *-us*: "wealth," "riches." **eximium:** "exceptional," "uncommon."

23 inpendamus = CL *impendamus* (pres. subj.) < *impendo*, *-ere*: "to put on," "apply."

24 tesauri = CL *thesauri*.

Uxor:

Tantum nefas, coniux, si fieret,
creatorem nimis offenderet,
et si quisquam forte perciperet,
nos per orbis spatium gereret
        infamia. 30

Respondeat hospes:

Frustra times. Bene celabitur,
nemo siet quod pertractabitur;
horum nobis morte parabitur
in manticis qui magnus clauditur
        opum census. 35

Uxor respondeat:

Fiat quod vis: ego consentiam,
que pro posse tibi subveniam;
tam infeste cladis nequitiam
caute tecum, coniuns, incipiam,
        uxor tua. 40

Speech 5: Innkeeper's Wife (26-30)

The innkeeper's wife reveals feelings of religious guilt and of anxiety over the shame that she and her husband would incur if discovered – all of which is aurally underlined by repeated "t" and "m". However, as Dronke (1994, 57) observes, "the fear of being brought to justice does not seem to enter her thought."

26 coniux = CL *coniunx*. **fieret** (impf. subj.) < *fio*, *fieri*: "to occur," "happen," "become," "be made," "be done."

28 forte: (adv.) "by chance."

29-30 nos . . . infamia = *infamia gereret nos per spatium orbis*; the personification of *infamia* recalls Vergil's similar depiction of *Fama* in the *Aeneid* (4.173-97), one of the most widely read works of Classical Latin literature in the Middle Ages. In addition, *infamia* stands out metrically since it is one of only two cases (the other is *diútius* in v. 60) where a four-syllable fifth verse in this play scans as an iamb followed by two unstressed syllables (i.e., *infámia*) rather than two trochees.

29 gereret (impf. subj.) < *gero*, *-ere*: "to carry."

Speech 6: Innkeeper (31-35)

The innkeeper attempts to win over his wife by dismissing her fears as trivial and by strongly appealing to her greed. The phrase *magnus . . . opum census* underscores his own insatiable greed and recalls the previous two occasions where he mentioned the students' wealth and his desire to possess it (22, 24-5).

31 celabitur < *celo*, *-are*: "to conceal."

32 siet = CL *sciet* < *scio*, *-ire*: "to know." **pertractabitur** < *pertracto*, *-are*: "to carry out."

33-5 horum nobis . . . census = *morte horum magnus census opum qui clauditur in manticis parabitur nobis*.

34 manticis < *mantica*, *-ae*: "knapsack," "backpack."

35 opum < *ops*, *opis*: "help," "aid"; (pl.) "resources," "wealth."

Speech 7: Innkeeper's Wife (36-40)

Although the innkeeper's wife quickly consents to her husband's wicked plan, she still denounces the monstrous deed. Her speech provides a brief glimpse into the (normative?) husband-wife relationship in the twelfth century. Despite her misgivings concerning the horrible act they are about to commit, she completely defers to her husband's wishes. Everything is for him – note the repeated references she makes to her husband (*tibi*, *tecum*, *tua*). She is the perfect medieval wife: loyal to her husband and supportive of all his actions, both good *and* bad.

37 que = *et*. **pro posse:** "as best I can."

38 infeste = CL *infestae* (gen. sing. adj. modifying *cladis*) < *infestus*, *-a*, *-um*: "hostile," "violent," "dangerous," "unsafe." **cladis** < *clades*, *-is*: "injury," "harm," "destruction," "crime." **nequitiam** < *nequitia*, *-ae*: "wickedness."

39 coniuns = CL *coniunx*.

Verba sancti Nicolai:

Ad te gradu nocturno venio,
tuo pauper amotus hostio—
hic exoro frui hospitio:
fave michi, pro Dei filio,
precor, hospes! 45

Respondeat hospes:

Intra cito meum hospitium,
ut per noctis istius spatium
meum tibi prosit auxilium:
quod exigis habe remedium—
vade sessum. 50

Nicolaus:

Nove carnis si quidquam habeas,
inde michi parumper tribuas,
quam si michi prebere valeas,
adiuro te per Deum, nequeas
plus placere. 55

51-4 Nove . . . nequeas: the metrical variation employed in these lines is quite unusual in two respects: (1) there are no dactyls that begin the second half of each verse. Instead, the second half of the four verses scan as follows: *sí quídquam . . .*; *parúmper . . .*; *prebére . . .*; *pér déum . . .*; (2) the first half of 54, *adiúro té*, consists of two iambs, a unique scansion for this part of the line in the play.

Speech 8: St. Nicholas (41-45)

Nicholas arrives during the same night claiming that he is a poor man who had been driven away from the inn – presumably because of his beggarly appearance – at some earlier date. He humbly begs for lodging, appealing to the innkeeper in the name of "God's son." The vowel "o" (13x), both long and short, is especially prominent in this stanza and may indicate Nicholas' (feigned) sorrowful state in his attempt to elicit sympathy from the innkeeper.

41 gradu < *gradus*, *-us*: "step."

42 tuo . . . hostio = *pauper amotus hostio tuo*; the entire phrase is in apposition to the "I" of v. 41. **amotus** < *amoveo*, *-ere*: "to drive from." **hostio** = CL *ostio* < *ostium*, *-i*: "door," "gate."

43 frui < *fruor*, *frui* (+ abl.): "to enjoy."

44 fave < *faveo*, *-ere* (+ dat.): "to support," "help," "give shelter to." **michi** = CL *mihi*.

Speech 9: Innkeeper (46-50)

As he did with the students, the innkeeper in his reply to Nicholas exudes charitable concern (and again his words are suffused with the "m" sound that was so prominent in his earlier speech in 16-25). This speech contains, perhaps, the only weakness of plot motivation in the play, for why should the innkeeper now decide to welcome the beggar whom he had earlier rejected? Is it due to feelings of guilt at his recent murder of the students? Is he thus trying to atone in some small way for his criminal actions? Or has the innkeeper lost all moral scruples and is now contemplating murdering future guests, both rich and poor, in order to obtain whatever wealth they possess?

46 intra < *intro*, *-are*: "to enter."

48 prosit < *prosum*, *prodesse*: "to benefit," "help."

49 quod exigis habe remedium = *habe remedium quod exigis*. **exigis:** < *exigo*, *-ere*: "to require," "need." **remedium:** "comfort," "cure."

50 vade sessum: synonymous with *Ite sessum* (v. 20).

Speech 10: St. Nicholas (51-55)

Nicholas is suddenly transformed from a poor, meek stranger into a haughty, bold aristocrat (note especially the repeated *michi* in the same position in two successive lines and the use of the plosives "p", "pr", and "pl"). Once inside he demands "fresh meat" – as if he were a wealthy nobleman who could afford the best (there is also a gruesome – and effective – allusion in this phrase to the students' corpses). This stanza contains several metrical and aural anomalies (see notes below the text) that seem to reflect Nicholas' metamorphosis.

51 Nove = CL *Novae* < *novus*, *-a*, *-um*: "new," i.e., "fresh."

52 parumper: (adv. as adj.) "a little bit," "a small portion." **tribuas** < *tribuo*, *-ere*: "to give"; this is the only instance in the play where the two-syllable end rhyme (in this stanza "e-as") is broken.

53 prebere = CL *praebere*: "to offer," "provide." **valeas** < *valeo*, *-ere*: "to be able," "can."

54 nequeas < *nequeo*, *-ere*: "to be unable," "cannot."

55 plus placere = *plus placere* <*mihi*>.

Respondeat hospes:

Quam tu possis, hospes, non habeo,
nec hanc tibi prebere valeo:
non sum dives set pauper maneo—
multis enim semper indigeo
        diutius.   60

Sanctus Nicolaus:

Falsum refers adque mendatium!
Nuper enim per infortunium
peregisti opus nefarium,
clericorum fundens exitium
        per corpora;   65

56-8 Quam . . . dives: the scansion of the first half of 56-8 (where the first two words of each verse are monosyllabic) is identical: a spondee followed by a trochee (i.e., three stressed syllables followed by one unstressed syllable). The effect of such "heavy" repetitive scansion hammers home the innkeeper's claim of poverty to Nicholas.

61-4 Falsum . . . exitium: these verses possess an unusual metrical regularity: two trochees + two dactyls. In fact, this is the only stanza in the play without any metrical variation. Note too the repetition (*Falsum...mendatium*; which is also an example of chiasmus) and strong consonance ("m", "n", "per"/"por"). Such rhetorical devices suggest a man who, though deeply angry, is not wildly emotional. Instead of shouting at the innkeeper, Nicholas is seen as an agent of God who attempts to impart to the perpetrator the severity of the crime that he has committed. Nicholas also conveys to his host that he knows how the murder was carried out. An important moral is thus presented to the innkeeper and to the audience: God's knowledge is absolute and no human action can ever be kept hidden from him. One recalls the innkeeper's wife's misgivings about her husband's criminal plan in vv. 26-7: *Tantum nefas . . . creatorem nimis offenderet*. This stanza vividly presents the response of God (via one of his agents on earth) to such a monstrous crime.

Speech 11: Innkeeper (56-60)

In reply to the beggar's demand for an expensive meal, the innkeeper repeatedly claims that, since he is a "poor man" (v. 58; cf. v. 42) and has been so for quite some time, he is unable to grant his guest's request.

56 possis = CL *poscis* (cf. *deposimus* in v. 14). **hospes:** here = "guest," "stranger"; the innkeeper's use of this word in its alternative meaning is ironic, for he unknowingly calls Nicholas what he himself should be but is not – a true "host" who shows "hospitality."

58 set = CL *sed.*

59 indigeo < *indigeo*, *-ere* (+ abl.) "to be in need of," "lack."

Speech 12: St. Nicholas (61-75)

In reply, Nicholas immediately and vehemently denounces the innkeeper and then, very abruptly, holds out to him (and presumably his wife) the opportunity for God's forgiveness. Somewhat surprisingly, Nicholas then aligns himself with the host as if he too were one of the guilty, and prays to God both for their own forgiveness and for the restoration to life of the murdered students. These three stanzas are the climax of the play – one that is achieved by the playwright not only verbally in his exposition of the nature of Christian forgiveness, but also through various literary and (especially) metrical techniques.

61 refers: *fero* and its compounds can also mean "say," "report," "tell." **adque** = CL *atque*. **mendatium** = CL *mendacium*.

62 nuper: (adv.) "recently," "not long ago." **per infortunium:** "calamitously."

63 peregisti < *perago*, *-ere*: "to perpetrate," "accomplish."

64-5 clericorum . . . per corpora: from these two verses it seems clear, as Dronke (1994, 77) notes, "that the innkeeper killed the three students by means of poison, perhaps like Claudius with King Hamlet, by pouring poison into their ears."

ergo prece mentis sollicite
nostro simul pectora tondite,
et dominum mecum depossite
indulgere nobis illicite
        crimen mortis! 70

Oratio sancti Nicolai:

Miserere nostri, rex glorie
nobis locum concede venie
et clericis peremtis impie
per virtutem tue potentie
        redde vitam! 75

Chorus:

O Christi pietas,
omni laude prosequenda,
qui sui famuli Nicolai merita
longe lateque mirabiliter declarat!

Angelus:

Nicolae, vita fidelibus 80
reddita est a Deo tuis precibus!

---

68 et dominum: the scansion of *ét dóminum*, though not unique in the play – the first half of vv. 34, 49, and 73 are identical to it – is quite striking here, for it is only in this phrase that the extremely regular metrical pattern of this stanza (two trochees + two dactyls; the same pattern that held throughout the preceding stanza) is disrupted. Thus the playwright directs the spotlight on God as "lord/master."

71-3 Miserere . . . impie: the variety of metrical patterns in these verses that begin Nicholas" prayer contrasts greatly with the metrical regularity of the previous two stanzas:

v. 71 = *Míserére nóstri réx glórie*
v. 72 = *nóbis lócum concéde vénie*
v. 73 = *ét clréricis perémtis ímpie*

Metrical "normalcy" – two trochees + two dactyls – is restored in v. 74.

66 prece < *prex*, *precis*: "prayer." **sollicite** = CL *sollicitae* < *sollicitus*, *-a*, *-um*: "troubled," "anxious."

67 nostro simul: "at the same time <I beat> mine." **tondite** = CL *tundite* < *tundo*, *-ere*: "to beat." **depossite:** see note to *deposimus* at v. 14.

69 indulgere: (+ dat.) "to pardon." **illicite** = CL *illicitae*.

71 Miserere < *miseror*, *-ari* (+ gen.): "to pity," "have mercy on." **glorie** = CL *gloriae*.

72 venie = CL *veniae* < *venia*, *-ae*: "pardon."

73-5 peremtis . . . vitam: the conclusion of the prayer employs heavy alliteration (especially "p", "t" and "m").

73 peremtis = CL *peremptis* < *peremo*, *-ere*: "to kill," "murder."

74 tue potentie = CL *tuae potentiae*.

75 redde < *redeo*, *-ire*: "to return," "give back," "restore."

Conclusion: Choir and Angel (76-81)

At the end the play reenters the world of the church as the choir sings in praise of Christ; this is followed by an "epilogue" in which an angel declares that Nicholas' prayer was answered.

77 prosequenda: <*quae* [i.e., *pietas*] *est* > *prosequenda* (a passive periphrastic); *prosequenda* < *prosequor*, *-i*: "to honor."

78 qui: <*Christus*> *qui*. **famuli:** < *famulus*, *-i*: "servant."

80 Nicolae: (voc.) scan as four syllables.

80-1 vita . . . reddita est: cf. *redde vitam* (v. 75).

Danielis Ludus

(“The Play of Daniel”)

c. 1140-1180

“Daniel the Prophet.” *Nuremberg Chronicle*, fol. LXIv.

Introduction

1 Cathedral Schools[20]

During the eleventh and twelfth centuries Western Europe experienced an intellectual revolution that changed the course of civilization. The hallmark of this change – and the catalyst for future change – was the written word. What started in the tenth century as a trickle of government documents, individual transactions (wills, business records, etc.) and treatises on philosophy, theology, law, and medicine soon became a flood in the following centuries that has never abated. For the first time in centuries new works of literary creation were regularly committed to writing rather than transmitted orally.

This shift "from memory to written record" had a profound impact on a variety of social, political, and religious institutions. The influence of Aristotelian logic in particular spread throughout society and imposed a more systematic approach to many aspects of human life. Businesses, farms, and kingdoms were now managed differently. Philosophical investigation and theological speculation were promoted and carried out on a level that had not been seen since the time of late antiquity. Perhaps not so surprisingly, it was the young who, seeing that, in Hollister's words (1982, 290-1), "the ability to reason, read, and calculate provided a direct avenue into the government institutions of church and state," first realized "that knowledge was power."

To cater to this new thirst for education schools sprang up throughout Western Europe, and the demand for teachers quickly outstripped the supply. The same economic prosperity that had contributed to the growth of urban centers such as Paris conversely brought about the decline of the old monastic schools, which had been the great caretakers of classical knowledge and literature over the previous centuries. The monasteries were superseded as centers of education, especially in northern France, by schools centering on cathedrals, many of which became renowned institutions of higher learning (e.g., Chartres, Paris).[21] The enrollments of these schools increased dramatically in the twelfth and thirteen centuries to such an extent that several of them evolved into universities (e.g., Paris, Montpellier, Oxford, Cambridge).

But it was in the cathedral schools in the first half of the twelfth century – not the later universities – where the genie of skeptical inquiry, armed with the rigorous tools of logic wielded by an increasing number of young disciples, first had been let out of the bottle. And it was this skepticism, further nurtured in the thirteenth-century universities by translations of many additional works of Aristotle which were previously unavailable, that would transform the politics, religion, art, music and literature of European civilization in the centuries to come.

---

[20] I am indebted in this section to Hollister 1982, 290-3.

[21] For the curriculum of these schools, see p. 17 fn. 19.

2 *Danielis Ludus*

(*i*) A School Text

In the intellectual revolution of the eleventh and twelfth centuries it was the teacher who became the focus of higher education. Those who demonstrated verbal acumen, a readiness to challenge older ideas and beliefs, and an ability to perceive new trends in society quickly acquired cult followings of students – and the fear and denunciation of the religious authorities.[22] Nowhere is this better exemplified than in the career of the most celebrated of all twelfth-century teachers, Peter Abelard (1079-1142). Self-centered, arrogant, hypercritical and possessing a brilliant mind, Abelard infuriated traditionalists, like Bernard of Clairvaux, by applying the principles of dialectical reason to the Bible. His itinerant career cut a wide and deep intellectual swath throughout France that left in its wake a host of students who soon became teachers themselves. One such Abelard protégé was Ralph of Beauvais, an Englishman whose name transparently discloses the school at which he achieved his greatest fame.

Although today Beauvais is one of the minor towns of France (*c*. 55,000 inhabitants), in the twelfth century it was a prosperous, cosmopolitan center of musical and artistic creativity that had the desire and the resources to attract a teacher of Ralph's stature.[23] Famous as an authority in classical and religious literature, Ralph taught at Beauvais cathedral school in the mid-twelfth century. It is perhaps more than a coincidence that the date most commonly assigned to the composition of the *Danielis Ludus* (*c*. 1140-1180) by the majority of scholars[24] corresponds with the time of his tenure at the school. Indeed, Emmerson (1996, 45) may be right in hypothesizing that Ralph of Beauvais taught the student (or students[25]) who composed the *Danielis Ludus*.

---

[22] Incidentally, the teachers were not in the employ of these schools but lived off the fees that they could draw from their pupils.

[23] Today the town of Beauvais is best known for its towering cathedral, whose construction began in 1225. Desiring to erect an edifice that would attest to the rest of Europe their unparalleled faith and great wealth, the civic and religious leaders of Beauvais built a lofty structure without regard to either cost or the laws of engineering. At its apex the choir vault reached 157 feet 6 inches (about three and a half times its span) – making the cathedral the tallest in Europe. Needless to say, the vault collapsed in 1284 shortly after the choir had been completed in 1272. The cathedral one now visits remains a truncated (albeit magnificent) fragment of its original design, and Beauvais, the fastest growing and richest city in France after Paris in the mid-thirteenth century, quickly went into decline as the cost of building (and rebuilding) the structure placed an irreparable strain on its economy. Nothing as great as Beauvais Cathedral was ever again attempted in Medieval France.

[24] For a list of the dates assigned by different scholars to the play, see Emmerson 1996, 59 n. 45. Emmerson does not include Dronke, the play's most recent (and best) editor, who (1994, 119) posits *c*. 1140.

[25] I shall refer to the author of the *Danielis Ludus* in the singular, though it is possible that the text was a collaborative project of the scholars of Beauvais cathedral school. Verse 2, in fact, tells us that the "inventors" of the play were "the young" (*iuventus*), a term which in the twelfth century included anyone between the ages of 21 and 50. The use of the collective noun *iuventus*, however, was often simply a convention, and neither precludes single authorship nor supports multiple authorship.

(*ii*) Pedagogy and Entertainment

Though written by a scholar, the composition of the *Danielis Ludus* was not an academic exercise. Instead, the text was a work meant for public performance in the cathedral and churches in and around Beauvais during the joyous celebrations between Christmas and Twelfth Night (Dec. 25-Jan. 6[26]). The liturgical drama that was performed during these festive holy days was meant to function effectively as both pedagogy and entertainment. As to the former, the *Danielis Ludus* and plays like it were an important part of the medieval church's need to keep the people in touch with the great and awe inspiring doctrinal mysteries.[27] With respect to the latter, it presented an opportunity for musical expression of a different kind to men and boys who normally sang the liturgy in the cathedrals and schools. In fact, the sheer joy of the chorus members at having the opportunity to perform non-liturgical songs is clearly evident throughout the text (cf. 28-9, 40-1, 61-2, and especially 132-3). What is less well known is the reaction of the audience to such dramas. However, the combination in this particular work of a sophisticated text with colorful, celebratory, and sometimes raucous music and dance strongly suggests that its performances were successful with both the cultivated elite and the general public of Beauvais.[28]

(*iii*) Old Testament Myth and Prophecy

The anonymous playwright of the *Danielis Ludus* based his drama on selected narratives from the book of *Daniel*[29], an Old Testament collection of mytho-historical stories and apocalyptic literature that was written down sometime in the middle of the year 164 BCE during a period of social and religious upheaval. This turmoil was precipitated by the Hellenistic Seleucid king Antiochus IV who, siding with the Hellenized Jews in their conflicts with the observant Jews, vigorously repressed the religious practices of the observant Jews and installed a pagan altar in the Temple in 167 BCE. This action led to the Maccabean revolt, a series of successful military campaigns that wrested control from the

---

[26] These are the "Twelve Days of Christmas." January 6 was the date on which the Feast of the Epiphany was celebrated, which commemorated the manifestation of Christ to the Gentiles in the persons of the wise men (*Matthew* 2.1-15).

[27] The *Danielis Ludus* may have had another, more pragmatic purpose: to divert the energies of the young scholars and lower orders of clergy from "inappropriate" behavior committed during the Feast of Fools (for additional information on this Feast, see **Appendix A**).

[28] Since the laypeople of Beauvais knew little Latin, they did not fully understand the liturgy and therefore could not learn from it all the teachings of the scriptures. Thus the liturgical dramas supplemented the liturgy by revealing to them many of the Bible's lessons. Despite the inclusion of the vernacular from time to time, the language barrier, Browne (1959, vi) asserts, "must have only truly been broken through by the visual and emotional impact of the acting – which introduced a new experience in church-going – and by the power of the music."

[29] There is also another play based on the Old Testament book of *Daniel* entitled "Story of Daniel for Performance" that was composed by Hilarius of Orléans (another of Peter Abelard's students) around 1130. Scholars, however, are divided on the question of influence. For bibliography on this issue, see Emmerson 1996, 57 n. 29 and Dronke 1994, 119.

Hellenistic Seleucid overlords of Judea and led to the rededication of the Temple in December 164 BCE.[30]

Daniel himself is a legendary figure of wisdom and righteousness that features in *Ezekiel* 14.14 along with the Old Testament characters Noah and Job. Thus it seems clear that the eponymous text chronicling the adventures of this sage was published with this pseudonym for two reasons: (1) to support the sufferings of the writer's contemporaries under the guise of praising the faithfulness of those in the past to the one God; (2) to confirm the remarkable prophecies related therein.[31]

The first six chapters of *Daniel* contain the popular folktales of the "Burning Fiery Furnace," "Belshazzar's Feast," and the "Lions' Den" – stories that contrast the foolish pride of the Babylonian kings with the devoted piety of faithful Jews. This piety would have been considered exemplary by the book's audience – observant Jews who, like Daniel, were heroes of the faith that refused to compromise with idolatry.

The second group of six chapters takes the form of visions that purport to be predictions at the time of Babylonian supremacy (*c*. 600-575 BCE) of what would happen to the four kingdoms of Babylon, Media, Persia, and Greece. At the close of the text the culmination of all history is proclaimed with God reigning supreme over a kingdom of the saints (12.1-4). In this half of the work are to be found two famous prophecies – the great judgment of the kingdoms of the earth and the establishment of "one like a son of man" (7.13-4) and "the coming of an anointed one" (9.24-6)[32] – that later Christians believed heralded the coming of Christ. In addition, the Greek translation of *Daniel* made *c*. 100 BCE includes two more stories after chapter 12 – "Susannah" (chapter 13) and "Bel and the Dragon" (chapter 14) – that were incorporated into Jerome's Latin translation of the Bible used by

---

[30] *Daniel* is, incidentally, one of the few Old Testament texts that scholars can date securely. The fact that it was composed in 164 BCE makes it the latest of all the books of the Hebrew scriptures.

[31] Modern scholarship believes that the references in *Daniel* to the fates of the empires of Babylon, Media, Persia, and Greece are not prophecies at all, but the impression by a Jewish writer of the early second century BCE looking back at the past. In fact, the one actual prediction concerning the fate of Antiochus IV (in *Daniel* 11.45) does not correspond with historical fact.

[32] *Daniel* 7.13-4: "Then I was looking in the vision of the night, and look!, one like the son of man was coming with the clouds of heaven (*cum nubibus caeli quasi filius hominis veniebat*) . . . 14 And he gave to him power and glory and kingdom; and all peoples, nations, and languages will serve him; his power is an everlasting power, that will not pass away, and his kingdom one that will not be destroyed."; *Daniel* 9.24-6: "Seventy weeks are shortened concerning your people, and concerning your holy city that transgression may be finished, and sin may end, and iniquity destroyed, and everlasting justice be brought in, and vison and prophecy be fulfilled, and the saint of saints (*sanctus sanctorum*) be anointed. 25 Know, then, and take notice: from the going forth of the word to rebuild Jerusalem until the anointed one, the prince (*usque ad Christum ducem*), there will be seven weeks, and sixty-two weeks . . . 26 And after sixty-two weeks the anointed one will be killed, and the people who will deny him will not be his (*occidetur Christus*: *et non erit eius populus, qui eum negaturus est*). . . ." It should be noted that *Christus*, a transliteration from Greek (which in turn is a translation of the Hebrew word "messiah'), simply means "anointed one." It was only after Jesus' death that the word "Christ" became a name.

our playwright.[33] In fact, it was Daniel's exploits in these stories that led some early Christians to the view that the Old Testament prophet prefigured Christ.[34]

(*iv*) Poetic Technique and Music

(a) Narrative

Ignoring nearly all of chapters 7-12 (the apocalyptic section) of *Daniel*, and only alluding to chapters 1-4 (Daniel's dealings with Nebuchadnezzar) and 13-14 (the stories of Susannah and Bel and the Dragon), the author of the *Danielis Ludus* chose to develop the material of his play primarily from the two most dramatic episodes of the Old Testament text: Chapter 5, Daniel's dealings with Belshazzar (which correspond to vv. 1-153 of our play), and Chapter 6, Daniel's dealings with Belshazzar's conqueror, Darius (vv. 154-280). His selection of stories committed him to a bipartite structure that he exploits in such a way by replaying, but modifying, in the second half of the drama the main themes of the first: secular vs. religious power, piety vs. blasphemy, wisdom, prophecy, revelation, and faith.

Once the playwright had selected his material for dramatization he had to make creative choices about how it could be staged successfully. Transforming an Old Testament narrative into a viable stage work proved to be quite challenging for many of this writer's predecessors and contemporaries. Indeed, impressive in certain ways as some of these works are, their many theatrical and literary weaknesses have relegated the vast majority of them to the ivory tower, where they are occasionally studied by medievalists, linguists, and historians of the theater. The *Danielis Ludus*, on the other hand, has the distinction of being the first medieval mystery play to be revived in modern times.[35] As attested by the numerous public performances of this work in Europe and North America in the past thirty years, its popularity continues unabated.[36] Our author, then, unlike the majority of medieval playwrights of his time, was something of a visionary in his craft. To what elements of his creative genius can we attribute his play's continuing success? The three most important factors are an innovative use of the chorus, an unrivalled command of language and meter, and the brilliance of the musical score.

---

[33] Jerome's translation of the Bible, completed in 402 CE, is known as the *Vulgate*. The stories in *Daniel* 13 and 14 are considered canonical in the Eastern Orthodox and Roman Catholic Churches, but are included in the *Apocrypha* in the Protestant Churches.

[34] The first evidence for this is in the oldest Christian commentary on *Daniel*, that of Hippolytus of Rome (d. 235 CE).

[35] The *Danielis Ludus* received its first performance since the Middle Ages by Noah Greenberg's *New York Pro Musica* ensemble in New York City (at The Cloisters) in 1958. The performance was quite successful and Greenberg subsequently took the work on tour for several years throughout the United States and abroad.

[36] See Collins 1996 for a survey of performances of the *Danielis Ludus* in the years 1958-1995. In addition to being the most performed Medieval Latin mystery play in the world, it is also the most recorded (see **Appendix B** for a list of audio recordings of the *Danielis Ludus* currently available).

(b) Chorus

In many ways the playwright's imaginative and sophisticated use of the chorus is the key to understanding his work. Unlike the non-choral sections of the drama, which for the most part follow closely (though occasionally with significant alterations) the original biblical text, nearly all the choral songs are freely invented.[37] Within the bipartite structure of the play he includes, as Dronke (1994, 111) observes, "a series of choral lyrics as acclamations and processional songs (*conductus*) to accompany the entrances and exits of the protagonists."[38] The large number of these choruses in such a short work (less than an hour in playing time) is quite unusual.[39] Yet instead of falling into the trap of creating an oratorio-like drama, the strategically positioned choral sections provide a structural framework where dramatically static sequences (processions and arrivals) alternate with short, powerful episodes of action. In addition, the numerous and elaborately staged choruses visually, musically, and textually reproduce the pageantry and spectacle of the medieval court and the newly created cathedrals.[40]

The playwright also transcends historic time – but in a different way – through the two-part role he assigns to his chorus.[41] Ostensibly playing the parts of Babylonian courtiers, wise men, Persian Satraps and legates, the chorus members occasionally step out of these roles and become who they are in real life: the boys and scholars of Beauvais cathedral school. As the latter they interweave allusions and "prophecies" into their songs that connect the biblical story of Daniel to the coming of Christ in a celebratory manner appropriate to the Christmas season.

Finally, the dramatic function of the chorus changes in the second half of the play to an extent rarely seen in medieval drama of this period. Instead of reprising the role of Belshazzar's court functionaries who simply comment on the action of the play and carry out their king's orders, Darius' noblemen emerge as an independent character whose actions affect the plot. It is the chorus, in fact, who scheme against Daniel and force an unwilling Darius to sacrifice him to the lions. And it is the chorus (or at least certain members of it) who, at the end, are themselves sentenced to death and devoured by the lions. Indeed, the conspirators have what may be the most dramatic moment in the play when, standing naked at the edge of the lion-pit, they confess their guilt (268-70). Both their speech and the visually effective act of showing them without clothing are not in the

[37] Cf. vv. 3-20, 26-46, 55-62, 122-35, 136-152, 153-69, 194-206 and notes *ad loc*. The choral songs thus comprise 108 of the play's 280 verses (or 39% of the total).

[38] Incidentally, the same structural use of the chorus occurs in Stravinsky's 1928 opera-oratorio *Oedipus Rex*.

[39] Stevens 1980, 36-7.

[40] Ogden (1996a, 3) describes the theatrical setting thus: "Perhaps only the ancient Greek theater can be said to have matched the medieval church's awesome stone presence, its mystery of light and incense, its air of celebration, its echo of the human community at prayer and song, its compass of the quotidian and its reach toward the divine – and its invitation to performance."

[41] Fassler (1991, 100) calls this temporal perspective, "a nonlinear sense of time, an "all time". . .," and describes it as characteristic of twelfth-century liturgical art: "it is an art with a view of time, a time wherein all events can be seen at once, placed one on top of the other in layers, lined up, focused, and explained through Christ." For this nonlinear sense of time in medieval theater, see also Harris 1992, 101-3.

Old Testament narrative but have been freely composed by a playwright who had a sure sense of what works theatrically.

(c) A Bilingual Text

An interesting feature of the *Danielis Ludus* is its use of the two languages that were heard in Beauvais in the twelfth century: Latin, the language of the elite that was employed in Church and by the scholars of the cathedral school; Old French, the vernacular spoken by the citizens of Beauvais.[42] Although Latin predominates, snatches of Old French appear with some regularity and are at times interwoven with the Latin verses (cf., e.g., 75-6: *Vir propheta Dei*, Daniel, vien al Roi: / *veni*, *desiderat* parler a toi.). The effect of such bilingual sections on the original audience cannot be known with absolute certainty. Through a process of literary deduction, however, it seems that in certain parts of the play that contain this feature, the vernacular establishes an everyday, colloquial world that stands in opposition to that of the noble, Latin-speaking court.[43]

(d) Rhyme

Although the Beauvais playwright displays a sure command of the various traditional literary and rhetorical tropes such as alliteration, anaphora, and wordplay, his ability to make effective rhymes may be his most impressive verbal achievement. Since the variety of rhyme schemes found in this play is quite extensive, listed below is only a representative sample of those found in the text. A fuller list of the rhyme schemes in this play is included in the section on meter immediately following.

A. End Rhyme (e.g., 22-3):

Vos qui paretis meis vocibus,
Afferte vasa meis usibus.

B. Internal Rhyme with End Rhyme (e.g., 55-6):

Cum doctorum et magorum omnis adsit contio,
Secum volvit neque solvit que sit manus visio.

---

[42] This is yet another aspect (though entirely a coincidental one!) that the two texts have in common, since the Old Testament text of *Daniel* is also bilingual (2.4-7.28 is in Aramaic, the rest is in Hebrew). Our playwright, however, would probably not have known this since he relied on the monoglot Latin translation of the Old Testament.

[43] This observation was first made by Dronke 1994, 112, 114-5; Davidson 1996, 81, and Ogden 1996a, 2 also mention it in passing.

C. Internal Rhyme + Internal Rhyme with End Rhyme in Alternate Verses (e.g., 3-6):

Astra tenenti, cunctipotenti,
turba virilis et puerilis contio plaudit,

Nam Danielem multa fidelem
et subiisse atque tulisse firmiter audit.

(e) Meter[44]

Equal to his virtuoso performance in the field of rhyme is the author's metrical inventiveness. Indeed, this is perhaps the most sophisticated Latin dramatic text of the twelfth century with respect to accentual meter.[45] With the exception of the parytonic and/or proparytonic accents (those that, respectively, fall on the second-last and third-last syllable of a segment or line of verse), the scansion of the remaining syllables in each type of meter is highly flexible. Examples of each meter that highlight this flexibility follow. The verses of this play ought to be read out loud in order to appreciate their metrical expressiveness and intricate rhymes.

Notes on accentuation:

1. Both parytone (p) and proparytone (pp) accent marks are in bold face.

2. Syllables with normal stress (i.e., those in words that do not carry the parytonic or proparytonic accents in the segment or verse) are marked with an acute that is not in bold face.

3. Syllables within words that are trisyllabic or greater have their secondary stress marked with a raised caret (e.g., Dâniélis).[46]

---

[44] I am indebted in this section to Dronke 1994, 116-8, whose brief discussion of the meter of the *Danielis Ludus* draws on the detailed work of Avalle (1984, 1987).

[45] See pp. 14-15 (**3 Meter**) for a brief introduction to Medieval Latin accentual meter. In addition to his *tour de force* handling of accentual meter, the playwright of the *Danielis Ludus* also includes a few lines of classical quantitative meters (hexameters and a Sapphic strophe) at the end of his drama.

[46] Knowing which syllables receive secondary stress in multisyllabic words is a difficult business that is compounded by the change in pronunciation of Latin in the Middle Ages (which in turn differs over time and by region). Often the meter, if it is sufficiently regular, as in the case of the *Tres Clerici*, can be of some guidance. In the *Danielis Ludus*, however, where the meter fluctuates greatly, it is a task to discover where (and if) secondary stress occurs in certain words. Consequently, I have noted only those syllables that, by means of metrical and linguistic evidence, seem to me the *most likely* candidates to receive secondary stress.

I. "Dialogue" Meters

<u>Verses</u> — <u>Metrical Scheme</u>

1-2, 233: 8p + 8p

1 = Ád honórem túi, Chr**í**ste, Dâniélis lúdus **í**ste
233 = Núnquan vóbis côncedátur quód vír sánctus síc perdátur.

22-5: 10pp

22 = Vós quí parétis méis v**ó**cibus,
23 = Afférte vása méis **ú**sibus

47-8, 50-2, 208-10
230, 252-5, 267: 8pp + 8pp

50 = Quí scriptúram hánc l**é**gerit ét sénsum âper**ú**erit,
51 = súb illíus poténtia subdétur Bâbyl**ó**nia,

64-73, 81-4, 120-1
120-1, 181-92, 212-
23, 256-8, 260-1: 4p + 6pp

64 = Út scrib**é**ntis nóscas ing**é**nium,
66 = Cúm Iud**é**e capt**í**vis p**ó**pulis,

75-80: 6p + 5 alternating with 6pp + 4

75 = Vír prophéta d**é**i, *Daniel*, *vien al Roi*:[47]
76 = véni, des**í**derat *parler a toi*.

98-103: 11pp

101 = ét prescíre quódlibet absc**ó**nditum.
102 = Sí érgo pótes scriptúram s**ó**lvere,

122-35: 3 + 7p

122 = Sólvitur ín líbro Sâlom**ó**nis
123 = dígna laús ét cóngrua matr**ó**nis.

---

[47] *Daniel* in Old French is bisyllabic; *vien* monosyllabic.

Verses | Metrical Scheme

171-80: 6pp + 6pp

171 = Audíte, pr**í**ncipes regális c**ú**rie,
172 = quí léges r**é**gitis tocíus p**á**trie:

194-9, 201-6,
273-6: 8p + 7pp

273 = Écce vénit sánctus **í**lle, sanctórum sanct**í**ssimus,
274 = quém réx íste iúbet c**ó**li pótens ét fort**í**ssimus.

200: 3 x 7pp

200 = ín hóc natal**í**tio, Dâniél, cúm ga**ú**dio té laúdat héc c**ó**ntio.

224-5: 4p + 4p

224 = Égo m**á**ndo ét rem**á**ndo
225 = né sít spr**é**tum hóc decr**é**tum. [*O hez*! = extra-metrical]

226-9,
231-2, 234-5: 4p + 4p + 7pp

226 = Núnquid, D**á**ri, ôbserv**á**ri stâtuísti **ó**mnibus
228 = ní té d**é**um íllum r**é**um darémus le**ó**nibus?

236-7, 246-7: 5p + 5pp

236 = Sí sprévit l**é**gem quám stat**ú**eram,
237 = Déus quém c**ó**lis tám fid**é**liter

248-51: 8p alternating with 8p [+ 4pp?]

248 = Huíus réi nón súm r**é**us:
249 = mîserére méi, d**é**us – *eléyson*! [= extra-metrical?]

268, 272: 7pp + 6pp

268 = Mérito héc p**á**timur, quía pecc**á**vimus:
272 = âdor**á**ri i**ú**beo á cúnctis p**ó**pulis!

II. "Lyrical" Meters

As an example of the sophisticated combination of various meters and rhymes in the songs of the play (especially the choruses), the first song (3-20) is cited below in greater detail than the others, which are listed by schematic formula followed by a limited number of examples. Verses that contain internal and end rhyme have their rhyme schemes listed in lower case letters. Thus, aabbc = a couplet (two verses) consisting of five segments in which the final syllables of each of the first two segments have the same rhyme (aa), the final syllables of the next two segments have the same rhyme (bb), but different than that of segments 1-2 (aa), and the final syllables of the last segment (c) do not rhyme with anything in the preceding segments – though (c) may share a rhyme with the final syllables of the last segment of the preceding/following couplet. An asterisk signifies no rhyme in the verse segment.

Song	(Verses)	Rhyme Scheme	Metrical Scheme
1	(3-20)		5 x 5p

3-6 aabbc

3 = Ástra ten**é**nti cúnctipot**é**nti, (a, a)
4 = túrba vir**í**lis ét puer**í**lis cóntio pla**ú**dit (b, b, c)

7-10 *a **a

7 = Cónvocat **á**d se[48] Réx sapi**é**ntes, (*, a)
8 = grámata d**é**xtre quí síbi d**í**cant ênucle**á**ntes; (*, *, a)

11-14 **a*a

11 = Séd Dâni**é**li scrípta leg**é**nti móx patu**é**re (*, *, a)
12 = qué príus **í**llis claúsa fu**é**re; (*, a)

15-16 aabbb (weak rhyme)

15 = Caúsa rep**é**rta, nón sátis **á**pta, (a, a)
16 = déstinat **í**llum óre le**ó**num dîlacer**á**ndum; (b, b, b)

17-18 *a**a

17 = Séd, déus, **í**llos ánte mal**í**gnos (*, a)
18 = ín Dâni**é**lem túnc volu**í**sti ésse ben**í**gnos. (*, *, a)

[48] For the sake of the meter, *se* is not stressed.

Song	(Verses)	Rhyme Scheme	Metrical Scheme
1	19-20	aabbb	5 x 5p

19 = Huíc quóque p**á**nis, né sít in**á**nis, (a, a)
20 = míttitur **á** te[49], prépete v**á**te prandia d**á**nte. (b, b, b)

Song	(Verses)	Rhyme Scheme	Metrical Scheme
2	(26-45)	*a*a	2 x 8p + 6p (I) or 7pp + 6p, 8p + 6p (II)

I = 26-9, 32-3, 38-41, 44-45

26 = Iûbilémus Régi nóstro mágno ác pot**é**nti!
27 = Rêsonémus laúde d**í**gna vóce cômpet**é**nti!

II = 30-1, 34-7, 42-3

30 = Páter eíus d**é**struens Iûdeórum t**é**mpla
31 = Mágna fécit, ét híc r**é**gnat eíus pér exempla

Song	(Verses)	Rhyme Scheme	Metrical Scheme
3	(55-62)	aabccb	4p + 4 p + 7pp

55 = Cúm doct**ó**rum ét mag**ó**rum ómnis ádsit c**ó**ntio,
56 = sécum v**ó**lvit néque sólvit qué sít mánus vísio.

The internal rhyme scheme of these eight verses follows the sequence:

55 = aab, 56 = ccb, 57 = dde, 58 = ffe ...

Song	(Verses)	Rhyme Scheme	Metrical Scheme
4	(85-96)	aabbc*c	Three strophes with 2 x 8pp + 8pp (with internal rhyme), followed by the refrain 8p, 6pp + 6p.

85 = Híc vérus déi f**á**mulus, quém laúdat ómnis p**ó**pulus,
86 = Cuíus fáma prud**é**ntie ést nóta régis c**ú**rie.
87 = *Céstui mánda lí Roís p**á**r nos.*
88 = Paúper ét **é**xulans *én voís ál Roí p**á**r vos.*

Song	(Verses)	Rhyme Scheme	Metrical Scheme
5	(136-52)	*a*a*ab*b/ *a*a*a*ab*b	Alternation between three-and four-line strophes of 4p + 4p lines, followed by the refrain 4p + 7pp + 4p.

136 = Régis v**á**sa rêfer**é**ntes
137 = quém Iud**é**e trémunt g**é**ntes,
138 = Dâni**é**li âpplaud**é**ntes,
139 = gaûde**á**mus: laúdes síbi d**é**bitas rêferámus!

---

[49] For the sake of the meter, *te* is not stressed.

Song	**(Verses)**	**Rhyme Scheme**	**Metrical Scheme**
6	(153-69)	155-6 = aaa 157-164 = aabb 165-6 = aaabb	A pair of strophes 6pp + 7pp, 7pp (153-6) is followed (157-66) by a series of rhythmic variations on 5p, 6p, 6pp, and 7pp elements, and at last (167-9) by a strophe (2 x 4p + 4p + 7pp, then 4 + 6pp).

153 = Écce réx D**á**rius vénit cúm princ**í**pibus,
154 = nóbilis nob**í**libus,

157 = 5p + 6p, 158 = 6pp + 6pp, 159 = 5p + 6p, 160-1 = 7pp + 7pp,
162 = 5p + 6p, 163 = 5p + 7pp, 164-5 = 7pp + 7pp, 166 = 7pp + 7pp + 7pp.

167 = Símul **ó**mnes grâtul**é**mur, résonent ét t**ý**mpana,
168 = cytharí**s**te tángant c**ó**rdas, mûsicórum **ó**rgana
169 = résonent ád eíus prec**ó**nia!

Song	**(Verses)**	**Rhyme Scheme**	**Metrical Scheme**
7	(238-45)		238-41 = 2 x 6p + 5p, 9p 242-5 = 2 x 7p, 8p

238 = Héu, héu, héu! quó cásu s**ó**rtis
239 = vénit héc dampnátio m**ó**rtis?

242 = hec féra túrba f**é**ris?
243 = Síc, mé, Réx, pérdere qu**é**ris?

III. Classical Meters (based on syllabic quantity, not stress)[50]

Verses	Metrical Scheme
262-3, 265-6:	Hexameter

262 = Téne, putás, Daniél, sálvábit ut éripiáris

[50] Syllables marked with an accent are long; those unmarked are short.

Verses	Metrical Scheme
277-80:	Sapphic strophe

> Núntiúm vóbís fero dé supérnís:
> nátus ést Chrístús, dominátor órbís,
> Ín Bethleém Iúdé—sic enìm prophéta
> Díxerat ánte.[51]

(f) Music

Based on internal evidence one can surmise that musical instruments were probably employed in the performance of the play.[52] The music must be inferred from the vocal line (in the twelfth century instruments were often looked on as extensions of the voice or used to support or double the vocal lines). The role of instruments, however, was very likely secondary.

Unusual for a work of this time, the music of the *Danielis Ludus* has a distinct large-scale structural function. Davidson (1996, 84) observes that, "the music both accompanies and carries the action in the drama from moment to moment, from unrest to climactic tension to [the] finale in rest and revelation." The anonymous composer of the play's music (who may have been the playwright) achieves these effects by making use of the whole range of medieval plainsong: free-flowing melodies in the folksong (troubadour-trouvère) tradition contrast with rhythmically accentuated, varying forms of song akin to instrumental dance music. Simple recitatives move the action along and provide a dramatic counterpoint to the diversity of the melodies.[53]

The music also functions to characterize the main individuals, the various choruses, and the changing moods of both. For example, Belshazzar's vocal range is limited. The majority of his lines consist of rather prosaic recitatives (22-5, 47-8, 74, 98-103). The single exception is his final (and technically speaking only true) song (119-21), in which he, now repentant, rewards Daniel and orders that the sacred vessels he and his father had profaned be returned to the Jews. The music he sings in this brief song evinces a lyrical quality absent from his earlier speeches. Its melancholy mood seems to reflect the fear he now has of his own mortality.

---

[51] This Sapphic stanza contains some peculiar characteristics: the "o" in *fero* (v. 277) is short (normally long in CL); the first syllable of *Bethleem* is short and the word is disyllablic (the first "e" in the second syllable is not pronounced); the "i" in *sic* can be either long or short in ML (here it is short).

[52] Cf. the references to zithers/lutes (29, 168), percussion (167), and the generic term "musicians' instruments" (168).

[53] Stevens (1980, 36) notes that, "there are at least fifty distinct melodies in the play, unrepeated and untraced in other sources . . . Only the last item, the Christmas hymn *Nuntium vobis fero*, can be identified liturgically."

Daniel, on the other hand, sings almost exclusively songs imbued with lyrical melodies. These, however, vary significantly as they serve to characterize his many different roles: the innocent stranger summoned to court (81-4); the wise prophet sternly admonishing his king (104-18); the terrified loyal advisor who, sentenced to death, sings a lament charged with emotion (238-45).

It is the chorus, however, with its many different roles, that employs the widest range of musical styles: noblemen of Belshazzar's court joyously celebrating their king's power, reputation, and deeds (26-45, 136-52); boys and scholars of Beauvais cathedral school who narrate the story with a hymn-like song (55-62) or joyfully prophesy the coming of Christ in a boisterous, celebratory tune (194-206); fanatic courtiers of Darius maniacally celebrating their king's conquest of Babylon (153-69); scheming Satraps first pressuring their king into condemning Daniel to the lions' pit (226-9, 231-2, 234-5), and soon thereafter lamenting their own impending death (268-70).[54]

---

[54] Davidson 1996, 77-86 gives an informative overview of the music's function in the drama that is accessible even to non-musicians. Zijlstra 1996, 88-116 provides a performance edition of the text in modern musical notation.

Incipit *Danielis Ludus*

PROLOGUE

Ad honorem tui, Christe, Danielis ludus iste
in Belvaco est inventus, et invenit hunc iuventus.

ACT 1

SCENE 1

Dum venerit Rex Balthasar, principes sui cantabunt ante eum hanc prosam: 2a

Astra tenenti, cunctipotenti,
turba virilis et puerilis contio plaudit,

PROLOGUE (1-2)

The second line of the prologue gives the reader/listener an immediate sense of the text's verbal pyrotechnics: *inventus . . . invenit . . . iuventus*, a phrase which contains both internal rhyme ("ventus"), anaphora (*inventus . . . invenit*), double and triple alliteration ("in" and "ven", respectively), and wordplay with respect to the idea that "youth" (*iuventus*) "composed" (*inventus*) this play. Another key to understanding this work is embodied by the word *ludus*. In addition to meaning "drama," *ludus* also means "play" (in the non-theatrical sense), "spectacle" and "entertainment" – aspects of *ludus*' semantic domain that will underscore much of the seriousiousness of the work.

1 ad honorem: *ad* + acc., an EL/ML construction = CL *in* + acc.: "for (the purpose of...)."

2 est inventus: "was composed"; *invenio* literally means "I find," "I discover," and, as Wulstan (1976, ii) notes, "implies an act of compilation, arrangement, and refinement." To a certain extent this is what the author has done with his biblical source material.

SCENE 1 (2a-46)

The opening rubric (2a) states that the scene begins with a processional sequence (*prosa*) sung by the Babylonian Satraps at the entry of Belshazzar. The verses sung by these courtiers reveal them to be boys and scholars of Beauvais, for they proceed to summarize the plot of the drama (5-20).[55] The story itself begins with the King's first words, a brusque command to his court to bring out the Jewish sacred vessels for his use (21-5). A joyous song accompanied by much singing and dancing follows in which the chorus contrasts Jerusalem and Babylon, the holy, moral city of God and the profane, corrupt city of the oppressor (26-46). This is the first appearance of the drama's most important theme: secular vs. sacred authority.

2a Dum venerit: as in CL, contemporaneity ("while", "as long as") or expectancy ("until") may be expressed in ML by clauses introduced by *dum*. Unlike CL, either the indicative or the subjunctive (*venerit* is either fut. perf. act. indic. or perf. act. subj.) can occur in these clauses, with no difference in meaning. **Balthasar:** Belshazzar's name means "Bel has protected the kingship." Historically, he was the son of Nabonidus (556-539 BCE), the last Neo-Babylonian ruler. Never a king, he acted as regent for ten years during his father's absences. **principes:** < *princeps, -cipis*: "noble." **prosam:** "sequence"; this type of music was sung during mass between the alleluia and gospel reading. Sequences are dramatic poems that normally follow a rhyme scheme, as here.

3 cunctipotenti = LL word equivalent to CL *omnipotenti*.

4 virilis: "of men." **puerilis:** "of boys." **contio:** synonymous with *turba*. **plaudit:** Dronke (1994, 144) notes that, "*plaudere* can, according to context, suggest applause, stamping of feet, or dancing; the use of the specific term for dancing (*tripudia* 156, *tripudio* 165) during the entry of Darius suggests that Belshazzar's entry too will have been accompanied by dance as well as music."

---

[55] The idea of providing a synopsis of the play's action at the beginning of the narrative is largely contrary to a modern audience's expectations. In a medieval liturgical play, however, nearly the exact opposite was the case, for these writers expected their audience to know the general outline of the story, especially one based on the Bible. The talents of medieval playwrights were to be measured not so much in devising original plots with invented fictional characters, but in their ability to give an engaging presentation to a familiar story.

Nam Danielem multa fidelem 5
et subiisse atque tulisse firmiter audit.

Convocat ad se Rex sapientes,
gramata dextre qui sibi dicant enucleantes;

Que quia scribe non potuere
solvere Regi, ilico muti conticuere. 10

Sed Danieli scripta legenti mox patuere
que prius illis clausa fuere;

Quem quia vidit Balthasar illis prevaluisse,
fertur in aula preposuisse.

Causa reperta, non satis apta, 15
destinat ilium ore leonum dilacerandum;

Sed, Deus, illos ante malignos
in Danielem tunc voluisti esse benignos.

Huic quoque panis, ne sit inanis,
mittitur a te, prepete vate prandia dante. 20

Tunc ascendat Rex in solium, et Satrape ei applaudentes dicant:

Rex, in eternum vive!

5 multa: "many <trials>."

6 subiisse (quadsyllabic) < *subeo*, *-ire*: "to undergo," "endure," "suffer." **audit:** The subject of this verb is *turba virilis et puerilis contio*; *audit* is singular since it agrees with the nearer subject, *puerilis contio*, a collective noun.

8 gramata: "writing" (LL from the Greek). **dextre** = CL *dextrae*. **qui sibi dicant:** (a relative purpose clause) = *ut dicant sibi*. **enucleantes** < *enucleo*, *-are*: "to explain in detail."

9 Que = CL *Quae* (i.e., *haec*). **scribe** = CL *scribae*. **potuere** = *potuerunt* (*potuere* is a syncopated alternative form found in verse; cf. also *conticuere* in v. 10, *patuere* in v. 11, and *fuere* in v. 12).

10 ilico: (adv.) "at once," "immediately." **muti conticuere:** since the meaning of *muti* ("mute," "silent") is redundant with the verb *conticuere* (< *conticesco*, *-ere*: "to become silent"), it carries adverbial force. Translate: "They became utterly silent."

11 patuere < *pateo*, *-ere*: "to be clear," "be plain," "be manifest."

12 que* = CL *quae*. **clausa fuere** = *clausa erant* (< *claudo*, *-ere*: "to conceal," "hide"; in EL/ML the pluperfect tense – *fueram*, *fueras*, etc. – may be substituted for *eram*, *eras*, etc., with no difference in meaning).

13 Quem = *eum* (i.e., Daniel). **prevaluisse** = CL *praevaluisse* < *praevaleo*, *-ere* (+ abl.): "to have more power than," "surpass."

14 fertur: *fero* and its compounds can also mean "say," "report," "tell." **preposuisse:** CL *praeposuisse* < *praepono*, *-ere*: "to prefer (someone or something) to."

15 reperta < *reperio*, *-ire*: "to find," "invent," "devise." **satis apta:** "very just."

16 dilacerandum < *dilacero*, *-are*: "to tear to pieces"; in ML the gerundive is sometimes used as a fut. pass. part. (e.g., "going to be ...ed").

17-18 Sed . . . benignos = *Sed, Deus, voluisti illos ante malignos in Danielem tunc esse benignos*.

17 ante = CL *antea* (not to be confused with the preposition *ante*).

19 inanis: "empty," i.e., "hungry."

20 prepete = CL *praepete* < *praepes*, *-etis*: "swift-flying." **dante** (part.) < *do*, *dare*.

20a Satrape = CL *Satrapae*; Satraps were the governors of the provinces of the Persian Empire. Although *Daniel* 6.1 suggests that Darius appointed one hundred twenty satraps for his kingdom, Herodotus, a Greek historian writing in the fifth century BCE about the Persian Empire, states that there were only twenty. *Satrapae* is synonymous with *Principes* throughout the play.

21 Rex, in eternum vive!: this acclamation is a refrain throughout the play (cf. 49, 63, 97, 170, 207, 211, 264) as it was in *Daniel* (cf. 3.9, 5.10, 6.6, 6.21). **eternum** = CL *aeternum*.

Et Rex apperiet os suum dicens: 21a

Vos qui paretis meis vocibus,
Afferte vasa meis usibus
Que templo pater meus abstulit
Iudeam graviter cum perculit. 25

21a apperiet = CL *aperiet* < *aperio*, *-ire*: "to open."

22-5 Cf. *Daniel* 5.2: *praecepit ergo iam temulentus ut afferrentur vasa aurea et argentea, quae asportaverat Nabuchodonosor pater eius de templo, quod fuit in Ierusalem, ut biberent in eis rex, et optimates eius, uxoresque eius, et concubinae.* ("Therefore, after he [Belshazzar] had already become drunk, he ordered that the gold and silver vessels be brought out, the ones which Nebuchadnezzar his father had carried off from the temple that was in Jerusalem, so that the king and his nobles, his wives and his concubines, might drink from them."). Note how the playwright has effected small but important changes to his source material. Instead of a drunk Belshazzar, his king remains sober, and thus more responsible for his blasphemous actions. Note too the removal of the reference to the King's wives and concubines. The playwright has, in effect, medievalized (i.e., Christianized) Belshazzar by giving him only one wife and by removing references to any extramarital relationships. In addition, the playwright highlights Belshazzar's speech and character in several ways. First, his speech is framed by two lengthy choral songs (18 and 20 verses in length, respectively). Second, the rather prosaic meter of the king's four verses – all 10pp, a scansion that appears only here in the play – contrasts with the more sophisticated meter of the two choral songs (see the introductory notes in section (e) Meter for their respective metrical analyses). Finally, the repetition of the possessive pronoun *meus* in the same position in vv. 22-4 characterizes Belshazzar as a rather egocentric authoritarian who expects complete obedience from his subjects.

22 vocibus < *vox*, *vocis*: "voice," "word."

23 vasa < *vas*, *vasis*: "vessel."

24 Que** = CL *Quae*. **Pater meus:** the author of our playwright's biblical source is mistaken here, for the father of Belshazzar was Nabonidus. The sacred Jewish vessels were taken from the temple in Jerusalem by Nebuchadnezzar, whose rule and that of Belshazzar (who, as already mentioned in the note to v. 2a, was never a "king") were separated by those of three other kings.

25 perculit < *percello*, *-ere*: "to overthrow," "beat down."

Satrape, vasa deferentes, cantabunt hanc prosam ad laudem Regis: 25a

Iubilemus Regi nostro magno ac potenti!
Resonemus laude digna voce competenti!

Resonet iocunda turba sollempnibus odis!
Cytharizent, plaudant manus, mille sonent modis!

Pater eius destruens Iudeorum templa 30
Magna fecit, et hic regnat eius per exempla.

Pater eius spoliavit regnum Iudeorum;
Hic exaltat sua festa decore vasorum.

Hec sunt vasa regia quibus spoliatur
Iherusalem et regalis Babylon ditatur. 35

Presentemus Balthasar ista Regi nostro,
Qui sic suos perornavit purpura et ostro.

Iste potens, iste fortis, iste gloriosus!
Iste probus, curialis, decens et formosus.

Iubilemus Regi tanto vocibus canoris: 40
Resonemus omnes una laudibus sonoris!

26-45 Cf. *Daniel* 5.3: *tunc allata sunt vasa aurea, et argentea, quae asportaverat de templo, quod fuerat in Ierusalem: et biberunt in eis rex, et optimates eius, uxores et concubinae illius*. ("Then the gold and silver vessels were brought in, which he had carried off from the temple that was in Jerusalem: and the king and his nobles, his wives and his concubines, drank from them."). Davidson (1996, 80) notes that this chorus has musical echoes of a song entitled "Song of the Ass" that, "would have established a secular, even satiric context for [the processional song]; coupled with the accents of the poetry which drive the piece into a metrical rhythmic rendition, the piece achieves a kind of youthful vitality. Conversely," she adds, "Taylor (1977, 192) has perceived this item as being "jingly" and even silly." Rhetorically, the song is replete with repetition and anaphora (e.g., *Iubilemus Regi* 26, 40; *potenti . . . potestati* 26, 44; *laude . . . laudibus* 27, 41; *voce . . . vocibus* 27, 40; *Resonemus . . . Resonet . . . sonent . . . Resonemus* 27, 28, 29, 41; *Pater eius* 30, 32; *spoliavit . . . spoliatur* 32, 34; *iste* 38-9) that hammer home its central point: absolute praise for the all-powerful king.

26 Iubilemus (EL from Hebrew) < *iubilo, -are*: "to celebrate."

27 Resonemus laude digna = either *Resonemus <eum> laude digna* ("Let us proclaim him with deserved praise") or *Resonemus <facta> digna laude* ("Let us proclaim his deeds worthy of praise"). **competenti** (pres. part.) < *competo, -ere*: "to coincide with," "be adequate," "be suitable"; in ML = "harmonious," "corresponding."

28 iocunda = CL *iucunda* < *iucundus, -a, -um*: "joyous." **sollempnibus** = CL *sollemnibus*: "ceremonial." **odis:** (abl. pl.; LL from the Greek) "songs."

29 Cytharizent = CL *Citharizent* < *citharizo, -are*: "to play the cithara (a stringed instrument from ancient Greece that was modified and used both in the Roman and medieval worlds, where its shape and sound resembled that of a zither or lute)." **mille:** (indecl. adj.).

33 exaltat (LL) < *exalto, -are*: "to celebrate," "magnify." **decore** < *decus, -oris*: "glory," "honor," "splendor," "beauty."

34 Hec = CL *Haec*. **spoliatur** = *spoliatum est* (< *spolio, -are*: "to strip/rob/plunder X [acc.] of/from Y [abl.]"); the present tense is used for the sake of the rhyme scheme.

35 Iherusalem: (indecl. noun; here = nom.). **ditatur** < *dito, -are*: "to enrich," "make wealthy."

36 Presentemus = LL *Praesentemus* < *praesento, -are*: "to present." **Balthasar:** (indecl. noun; here = dat.; in v. 43 = acc.).

37 suos = *suos <homines>*. **ostro** < *ostrum, -i*: "scarlet."

39 probus, curialis: in ML mean, respectively, "gallant" and "courtly". Dronke (1994, 144) notes that, "in the acclamations, the protagonists are praised for their specifically courtly excellence. Thus Daniel (89f.) *in iuventutis gloria . . . satis excellit omnibus virtute, vita, moribus*, and Darius (163) is celebrated for *honestas* and *nobilitas*." By investing the Old Testament world with such sentiments the playwright modernizes the story for his audience.

41 una: (adv.) "together."

Ridens plaudit Babylon, Iherusalem plorat;
Hec orbatur, hec triumphans Balthasar adorat.

Omnes ergo exultemus tante potestati,
Offerentes Regis vasa sue maiestati. 45

Tunc principes dicant:

Ecce sunt ante faciem tuam!

SCENE 2

Interim apparebit dextra in conspectu Regis scribens in pariete: Mane, Thechel, Phares. *Quam videns Rex stupefactus clamabit*: 46a

42 plaudit: "leaps."

43 Hec* = CL *Haec*. **orbatur** < *orbo*, *-are*: "to make destitute." **hec** = CL *illa* (*hic* and *ille* are used interchangeably in ML).

43, 45 adorat . . . sue maiestati: *adoro* is used in the Old Testament primarily of worshipping God (e.g., *Genesis* 24.26, 42, 52; *Exodus* 4.31, 11.8, 12.27) and in the New Testament almost exclusively of worshipping Jesus and/or God (e.g., *Matthew* 2.2, 8, 11, 4.10, 8.2, 9.18, etc.; *Mark* 5.6, 15.19; *Luke* 4.8, 24.52; *John* 4.20-4 [10x], 9.38, 12.20). In the very few cases in the New Testament where *adoro* is not used of Jesus or God either Satan is tempting Jesus to worship him (*Matthew* 4.9, *Luke* 4.7) or the survivors of the plagues that have killed a third of humanity are worshipping demons and idols (*Apocalypse* 9.20). In this play the rubric at 62a states that his own queen worships (*adorabit*) Belshazzar in this manner, while the rubric at 225a (which very closely follows *Daniel* 6.10) states that after Daniel has learned of the decree forbidding him to worship any god but Darius he "will go into his house and adore (*adorabit*) his God." The word *maiestas* is normally applied to God in the Old Testament (e.g., *Isaiah* 3.8) and exclusively applied to either God (e.g., *Hebrews* 1.3, *Apocalypse* 15.8) or to Jesus (e.g., *Matthew* 19.28, 24.30 25.31 [*in maiestate sua*], 25.31; *Luke* 9.26 [*in maiestate sua*], 9.31, 32) in the New Testament. Such allusions as these indicate an act of impiety in the court's excessive worship of Belshazzar. And although the vast majority in the original audience would not have picked up on these allusions, they would have been noticed by at least some of those who had an intimate knowledge of the Latin Bible – the students, scholars, and clergy.

44 exultemus = CL *exsultemus* < *exsulto*, *-are* (here + dat.). **tante** = CL *tantae*.

45 sue = CL *suae*.

SCENE 2 (46a-74)

Whereas in *Daniel* 5.4 Belshazzar and his court drink from the Jewish vessels and praise "the gods of gold and silver, bronze, iron, wood, and stone," the Beauvais playwright eliminates these actions and immediately brings in the mysterious hand of doom (46a). This supernatural event precipitates a reaction in the king of such great fear that he immediately summons to his court all the wise men in his kingdom (46-9). Despite his promise of material rewards and great honor to the one who can reveal its ominous meaning to him, the various astrologers, diviners, soothsayers, and magicians reply that the interpretation of the writing eludes them (50-4). This parallels the biblical narrative rather closely. New is the processional song that accompanies the Queen's entrance (55-62; *Daniel* 5.10 simply stated that the "queen entered the banqueting hall."). Once again, in the midst of their song, the chorus steps out of their dramatic role and foreshadows the future in which a prophet will reveal to the king his fated death (59-60). The Queen then enters and tells the king about Daniel, a Jewish prophet taken captive by his father (an allusion to the events described in *Daniel* 1-4), who can reveal to them what the writing means (63-73).

46a Mane, Thechel, Phares: the Hebrew words were "Mene, Mene, Tekel, and Parsin" (the first "Mene" is believed to be a scribal error). In 1886, Charles Clermont-Ganneau suggested that the terms reflect ancient weights or measures: mina, shekel, and half-shekel; a view now widely held by scholars. The meaning of the inscription in *Daniel*, however, lies not in these nouns but in the verbal notions behind them: Belshazzar's kingdom was numbered (*mene*); he was weighed (*tekel*); his kingdom was divided (*parsin*) between the Medes and the Persians.

Vocate mathematicos, Caldeos et ariolos, 47
auruspices inquirite et magos introducite!

Tunc adducentur magi, qui dicent Regi:

Rex, in eternum vive! Adsumus ecce tibi.

Et Rex:

Qui scripturam hanc legerit et sensum aperuerit, 50
sub illius potentia subdetur Babylonia,
et insignitus purpura torque fruetur aurea.

Illi vero, nescientes persolvere, dicent Regi:

Nescimus persolvere nec dare consilium
que sit superscriptio, nec manus inditium.

Conductus Regine venientis ad Regem: 54a

Cum doctorum et magorum omnis adsit contio, 55
secum volvit neque solvit que sit manus visio.
Ecce prudens, styrpe cluens, dives cum potentia,
in vestitu deaurato coniunx adest regia.
Hec latentem promet vatem per cuius indicium
Rex describi suum ibi noverit exitium. 60
Letis ergo hec virago comitetur plausibus,
cordis, orisque sonoris personetur vocibus!

47-52 Cf. *Daniel* 5.7: *exclamavit itaque rex fortiter ut introducerent magos, Chaldaeos, et aruspices. Et proloquens rex ait sapientibus Babylonis*: *Quicumque legerit scripturam hanc, et interpretationem eius manifestam mihi fecerit, purpura vestietur, et torquem auream habebit in collo, et tertius in regno meo erit* ("And so the king cried out loudly to bring in the wise men, the Chaldaeans [or "astrologers"], and the soothsayers. And the king, addressing them, said to the wise Babylonians: "Whoever can read this writing and make its meaning clear to me will be clothed in purple and will have a gold neck-chain on his neck and will be the third man in my kingdom."")

47 mathematicos: "astrologers." **Caldeos:** since the Chaldaeans were famed for astrology, *Caldeus* is often a synonym for "astrologer"; otherwise, Chaldaean is simply another name for Babylonian. **ariolos:** (EL) "magicians," "diviners."

48 auruspices = CL *haruspices*: "soothsayers," "prophets" (who foretold the future from the inspection of the vital organs of animals). **magos:** "magicians," "wise men."

51 subdetur < *subdo*, *-are*: "to put under," "make subject."

52 insignitus: "robed." **purpura:** (abl.). **torque:** (abl.) "neck-chain," "collar." **fruetur** < *fruor*, *frui* (+ abl.): "to enjoy."

53-4 The syntax of these verses is rather loose, perhaps reflecting the wise men's fear of their king. Dronke's translation ("We don't know how to solve this or how to give advice on what the writing might be or what the hand might mean.") conceals some of the awkwardness of the lines. Contrast the reaction of the wise men here with their response in *Daniel* 5.8: *Tunc ingressi omnes sapientes regis non potuerunt nec scripturam legere, nec interpretationem indicare regi*. ("Then all of the king's wise men came in, but they could not read the writing nor explain to the king its meaning.")

53 consilium: "advice."

54 superscriptio: (LL) "writing." **manus:** (gen., as also in v. 56). **inditium** = CL *indicium* (cf. v. 59): "meaning," "sign."

54a Conductus: a *conductus* is a processional song. These dramatic *conductus* are related to the liturgical ones, whose purpose in the liturgy is to bring the reader of the lesson to the lectern. The play uses them for a similar reason: to introduce each character as he/she proceeds to his/her destination on stage. **Regine** = CL *Reginae*.

55 Cum . . . adsit: *cum* + subj. can be temporal or circumstantial (i.e., "when"), causal (i.e., "since"), or concessive (i.e., "though") in meaning. **doctorum** < *doctor*, *-oris*: "teacher," "wise man," "sage."

57 prudens: the queen is called *prudens* in the play because she is Babylon's only memory of God's prophet, Daniel. **styrpe** = CL *stirpe* < *stirps*, *-pis*: "family," "lineage," "race."

58 deaurato (LL) < *de* + *auratus*, *-a*, *-um*.

59 Hec** = CL *Haec* (i.e., the Queen). **promet** < *promo*, *-ere*: "to bring out." **indicium:** "unfolding," "disclosure."

60 describi < *describo*, *-ere*.

61 Letis = CL *Laetis* < *laetus*, *-a*, *-um*: "happy," joyful." **virago:** "mighty queen"; the reference is to Belshazzar's queen and/or the Virgin Mary.

62 oris < *os*, *oris*: "mouth," "voice," "speech" <of the crowd of those assembled here>. **sonoris:** (adj. dat. pl.). **personetur** < *persono*, *-are*: "to fill with sound," "cry out," "proclaim."

Tunc Regina veniens adorabit Regem dicens: 63a

Rex, in eternum vive!
Ut scribentis noscas ingenium,
Rex Balthasar, audi consilium. 65

Rex audiens hec versus Reginam vertet faciem suam. 65a
Et Regina dicat:

Cum Iudee captivis populis,
prophetie doctum oraculis,
Danielem, a sua patria
captivavit patris victoria.
Hic, sub tuo vivens imperio, 70
ut mandetur requirit racio.
Ergo manda ne sit dilatio,
nam docebit quod celat visio.

Tunc dicat Rex principibus suis:

Vos Danielem querite et inventum adducite.

SCENE 3

Tunc principes invento Daniele dicant ei:

Vir propheta Dei, *Daniel, vien al Roi*: 75
veni, desiderat *parler a toi*.
Pavet et turbatur—*Daniel, vien al Roi*
vellet quod nos latet *savoir par toi*.
Te ditabit donis—*Daniel, vien al Roi*
Si scripta poterit *savoir par toi*. 80

Et Daniel eis:

Multum miror cuius consilio
me requirat regalis iussio.

63-73 Contrast the queen's speech in the play with her counterpart in *Daniel* 5.10-12: "King, live for ever! Let not your thoughts disturb you or your complexion change. 11 There is a man in your kingdom who has the spirit of the gods in him, and in the days of your father knowledge and wisdom were found in him. And for this your father, king Nebuchadnezzar, appointed him chief of his wise men, enchanters, Chaldaeans (or "astrologers"), and soothsayers. Your own father, O king, <did this> 12 because a greater spirit and wisdom and intelligence and interpretation of dreams and revealing of secrets and solving of difficult things were found in him, that is, in Daniel, to whom the king gave the name Belshazzar. Therefore, let Daniel now be called for, and he will tell you the meaning."

64 ingenium: "mind."

66 Cum: "among." **Iudee** = CL *Iudeae.*

67 prophetie = EL (from the Greek) *prophetiae* < *prophetia, -ae*: "prophecy." **doctum** = *<virum> doctum*: "a man wise in..."

71 ut mandetur: "that he (Daniel) should be commanded <to come to you>." **racio** = CL *ratio.*

74 querite = CL *quaerite.* **inventum adducite:** unlike Latin, which is fond of participles, English idiom prefers to use a temporal or circumstantial clause. Therefore, translate *inventum* as "when he has been found."

SCENE 3 (74a-96)

To effect a more dramatic encounter between Daniel and Belshazzar, the playwright has eliminated the fact that in the original story Daniel had already been highly honored by Belshazzar's father, who had given him the exalted status as principal wise man of the court (*Daniel* 5.11). As now constructed, the scene develops the more dramatic idea of the stranger who, possessing nothing, comes to the court and is revealed to be the wisest and noblest man there. Thus the simple statement of the original text (5.13), "Then Daniel was brought in before the king," is transformed into an entire scene containing the noblemen's summons of Daniel and the processional song that accompanies his entrance before the king. This song develops a clear antithesis between the nobles' praise of Daniel's wisdom and beauty (85-6, 89-90, 93-4) and the humble portrait that Daniel paints of himself in his identical, single-verse responses (88, 92, 96).

75, 77, 79 *Daniel, vien al roi*: OF "Daniel, come to the King."

76-80 The subject of every verb in these verses is the king.

76 *parler a toi*: OF "to speak with you."

78 nos latet: "lies hidden from us."

78, 80 *savoir par toi*: OF "to know through you."

82 iussio = LL for CL *iussum.*

Ibo tamen, et erit cognitum
per me gratis quod est absconditum.

Conductus Danielis venientis ad Regem: 84a

Principes:

Hic verus Dei famulus, quem laudat omnis populus, 85
Cuius fama prudentie est nota regis curie.
Cestui manda li Rois par nos.

Daniel:

Pauper et exulans *en vois al Roi par vos*.

Principes:

In iuventutis gloria, plenus celesti gratia,
Satis excellit omnibus virtute, vita, moribus. 90
Cestui manda li Rois par nos.

Daniel:

Pauper et exulans *en vois al Roi par vos*.

Principes:

Hic est cuius auxilio solvetur illa visio,
In qua scribente dextera mota sunt Regis viscera.
Cestui manda li Rois par nos. 95

Daniel:

Pauper et exulans *en vois al Roi par vos*.

86 prudentie = CL *prudentiae*. **Curie** = CL *curiae* < *curia*, *-ae*: "court."
87, 91, 95 *Cestui . . . nos*: OF "The King has summoned this man through us."
88, 92, 96 *en vois al Roi par vos*: OF "I am off to the king, through you."
89 in iuventutis gloria: this phrase recalls the prologue's statement (v. 2) that "it was the youth of Beauvais who composed" this play. The author of our play clearly sympathized with his protagonist on several levels. Ogden (1996a, 2) argues that the composers (Ogden believes in multiple authorship) actually identified with Daniel, "[admiring] his resistance against misdirected authority and [his] ability to decipher what was hidden to rulers and wise men. They could also identify with his taking of risks and, snatched from the very jaws of death, his final vindication and triumph." Emmerson (1996, 39) simply notes that, "it is no matter that [Daniel] served kings ranging over several generations – he is consistently portrayed as a "juventus" ("young man") and "adolescens" ("youth") and is therefore a particularly appropriate role model for the youth of Beauvais." **plenus:** (+ abl.). **celesti** = CL *caelesti*.
90 Satis: "far," "by far."
94 scribente dextera: (abl. abs.).

SCENE 4

Veniens Daniel ante Regem, dicat ei:

Rex, in eternum vive!

Et Rex Danieli:

Tune Daniel nomine diceris,
huc adductus cum Iudee miseris?
Dicunt te habere Dei spiritum 100
et prescire quodlibet absconditum.
Si ergo potes scripturam solvere,
immensis muneribus ditabere.

SCENE 4 (96a-152)

For the first part of this scene (96a-119) the playwright abridges *Daniel* 5.16-29 and moves from a generalized description of Nebuchadnezzar's pride (*Daniel* 20) to a specific focus on his blasphemous desire to be God and to his looting of the Temple's sacred vessels. In the second part of the scene he invents Belshazzar's decision to return the vessels to the Jews (120-21). This contrasts sharply with the original narrative, which at this point in the story simply describes Belshazzar's end (5.30): "on that same night Baltasar the Chaldean king was killed." Belshazzar's command to return the plundered vessels is immediately followed by two *conductus*. The first (122-35) is the processional song that accompanies the queen's departure. In it the playwright equates the queen with the ideal wife described in *Proverbs* 31.10-11 as brave and virtuous (124-31). The song then moves into the present (132-5) as the chorus revels in its "opportunity to play" and devotedly sings praises to the Queen (i.e., the Virgin Mary) "on this ceremonial day." The second *conductus* (136-52) is sung by the Satraps as they return the sacred vessels. In their song they praise Daniel not only for deciphering the mysterious writing, but, rather surprisingly, also for his deliverance of the wronged Susannah – an episode that will occur only near the end of the biblical text (ch. 13). By displacing this reference from its traditional narrative position, the chorus members once again signal to us that they have stepped outside the dramatic framework of the play. Since Christians had long come to believe that Daniel prefigured Christ, they read into Daniel's actions microcosmic versions of Christ's own. Thus in celebrating Daniel as the savior of Susannah, they are actually celebrating Christ as savior of all.

98-100 Cf. *Daniel* 5.13-14: *igitur introductus est Daniel coram rege. Ad quem praefatus rex ait: Tu es Daniel de filiis captivitatis Iudae, quem adduxit pater meus rex de Iudaea?* 14 *Audivi de te quoniam spiritum deorum habeas: et scientia, intelligentiaque ac sapientia ampliores inventae sunt in te.* ("Then Daniel was brought in before the king. And the king spoke and said to him: "Are you Daniel of the sons of the captivity of Judah, whom my father the king brought out of Judea? 14 I have heard of you that you have the spirit of the gods, and that rather impressive knowledge and intelligence and wisdom are found in you."")

99 Iudee* = CL *Iudeae*.

101 prescire = CL *praescire*.

102-4 Cf. *Daniel* 5.16-17: *porro ego audivi de te, quod possis obscura interpretari, et ligata dissolvere: si ergo vales scripturam legere, et interpretationem eius indicare mihi, purpura vestieris, et torquem auream circa collum tuum habebis, et tertius in regno meo princeps eris.* 17 *Ad quae respondens Daniel, ait coram rege: Munera tua sint tibi, et dona domus tuae alteri da: scripturam autem legam tibi, rex, et interpretationem eius ostendam tibi.* (""But I have heard of you that you can interpret obscure things and solve problems. Therefore, if you can read this writing and tell me its meaning, you will be clothed in purple and you will have a gold neck-chain around your neck, and you will be the third ruler in my kingdom." 17 In reply Daniel said before the king: "Let your rewards be for yourself and give the gifts of your house to another man. However, I will <still> read this writing for you, O king, and I will reveal its meaning to you."")

103 ditabere: cf. v. 35 (*ditabere* is an alternative form of *ditaberis*).

Et Daniel Regi:

Rex, tua nolo munera: gratis solvetur litera;
est autem hec solutio: instat tibi confusio. 105
Pater tuus, pre omnibus potens olim potentibus,
turgens nimis superbia, deiectus est a gloria.
Nam cum Deo non ambulans, sed sese deum simulans,
vasa templo diripuit, que suo usu habuit.
Sed post multas insanias tandem perdens divitias, 110
forma nudatus hominis, pastum gustavit graminis.
Tu quoque, eius filius, non ipso minus impius,
dum patris actus sequeris, vasis eisdem uteris!
Quod quia Deo displicet, instat tempus quo vindicet,
nam scripture indicium minatur iam supplitium. 115
Et "Mane", dicit dominus, est tui regni terminus;
"Thechel" libram significat que te minorem indicat;
"Phares", hoc est divisio, regnum transportat alio.

Et Rex:

Qui sic solvit latentia ornetur veste regia.

104 litera = CL *littera* (synonymous with *scriptura*).

105 solutio: CL = "loosening"; "payment"; ML = "solution." **confusio:** "trouble," "disaster."

106-9 Cf. *Daniel* 5.20: *quando autem elevatum est cor eius, et spiritus illius obfirmatus est ad superbiam, depositus est de solio regni sui, et gloria eius ablata est*. ("But when his heart was lifted up and his spirit hardened in pride, he was deposed of his kingdom's throne and his glory was taken away.")

106 pre = CL *prae*.

107 The sentiment, vocabulary, and imagery of this verse are those normally used in medieval literature to describe the fall of Satan (in this edition, cf. v. 87 of Hildegard's *Ordo Virtutum*, where the Virtues tell the Devil: *quia, inflatus superbia, mersus es in gehennam*). **turgens** = "swollen."

108 cum Deo non ambulans: the phrase "walking with God" is used of Enoch (*Genesis* 5:22, 24 *et ambulavit Enoch cum Deo*) and Noah (*Genesis* 6.9: *Noe vir iustus atque perfectus fuit in generationibus suis cum Deo ambulavit*) in the Old Testament: two men who were said to have lived holy and just lives in accordance with God's commands. **sese deum simulans**: cf. note to vv. 43, 45 above. **sese:** intensive form of *se*.

110 insanias < *insania, -ae*: "madness"; (pl.) "insane acts."

111 forma nudatus hominis: "stripped of human form." **pastum gustavit graminis:** cf. *Daniel* 5.21: "And he was cast out from the sons of men, and his heart was made like the beasts, and his home was with the wild asses, and he also ate grass like an ox, and his body was wet with the dew of heaven, until he knew that the Most High <God> held power in the kingdom of men, and that he will set over it whomever he wishes."

112 Cf. *Daniel* 5.22: *tu quoque filius eius Baltassar, non humiliasti cor tuum, cum scires haec omnia* ("You too, his son, Baltassar, have not humbled your heart, although you knew all these things.").

113 dum: CL "while" is also used in ML (with an indic. or subj. verb) either to mean "since" or to describe manner or means (e.g., "by ...ing"). **actus:** (acc. pl.).

114 tempus quo vindicet: (subject of *instat*) "the time when he takes vengeance."

115 scripture = CL *scripturae* < *scriptura, -ae*: "writing." **supplitium:** CL *supplicium* < *supplicium, -i*: "punishment."

116-8 Cf. *Daniel* 5.26-8: *et haec est interpretatio sermonis. MANE: numeravit Deus regnum tuum, et complevit illud*. 27 *THECEL: appensus es in statera, et inventus es minus habens*. 28 *PHARES: divisum est regnum tuum, et datum est Medis, et Persis*. ("And this is the meaning of the writing: MENE: God has numbered <the days of> your kingdom and has brought it to an end. 27 THECEL: you have been weighed in a balance and have been found wanting. 28 PHARES: your kingdom is divided and is given to the Medes and the Persians.")

117 libram < *libra, -ae*: "balance," "scales." **minorem:** "lesser <in moral weight than you ought to be to balance the scales>."

119 latentia: "the things lying hidden," i.e., "the riddle of the writing." **ornetur veste regia:** cf. *Daniel* 5.29: "Then at the king's order Daniel was clothed in purple and a golden chain was placed around his neck, and it was proclaimed of him that he should hold the third power in the kingdom."

Sedente Daniele iuxta Regem, induto ornamentis regalibus, exclamabit Rex ad principem militie: 119a

Tolle vasa, princeps militie, 120
ne sint michi causa miserie.

Tunc, relicto palatio, referent vasa satrape. Et Regina discedet. Conductus Regine: 121a

Solvitur in libro Salomonis
digna laus et congrua matronis.
Precium est eius, si qua fortis,
procul et de finibus remotis. 125
Fidens est in ea cor mariti,
spoliis divitibus potiti.
Mulier hec illi comparetur,
cuius Rex subsidium meretur.
Eius nam facundia verborum 130
arguit prudentiam doctorum.
Nos quibus occasio ludendi
hac die conceditur sollempni,
Demus huic preconia devoti,
veniant et concinent remoti! 135

Conductus referentium vasa ante Danielem: 135a

Regis vasa referentes
quem Iudee tremunt gentes,
Danieli applaudentes, gaudeamus:
laudes sibi debitas referamus!

Regis cladem prenotavit 140
cum scripturam reseravit;
testes reos comprobavit
et Susannam liberavit—gaudeamus:
laudes sibi debitas referamus!

119a militie = CL *militiae*.

121 michi = CL *mihi*. **miserie** = CL *miseriae*.

121a relicto palatio: (abl. abs. referring to the King). **Satrape*** = CL *Satrapae*. **Regine*** = CL *Reginae*.

122 Solvitur < *solvo*, *-ere*: "to untie," "free," "unlock." **in libro Salomonis:** the "Book of Solomon" is *Proverbs*, an Old Testament text considered by ancient and medieval Christians to have been composed by king Solomon, who ruled Israel *c*. 962-922 BCE. Modern scholars, however, believe that *Proverbs* was composed after the Babylonian Captivity (586-536 BCE). *Proverbs* is a collection of pithy sayings and moral advice for the instruction of the young.

124-7 Cf. *Proverbs* 31.10-11: *mulierem fortem quis inveniet procul et de ultimis finibus pretium eius*. 11 *confidit in ea cor viri sui et spoliis non indigebit*. ("Who will find a brave wife? Far off and from the farthest lands is her excellence. 11 The heart of her husband trusts in her, and he will have no need of spoils.")

124 Precium = CL *Pretium*: "excellence," "price."

124-5 est . . . procul: "is far," i.e., "travels far."

126 Fidens . . . mariti = *cor mariti est fidens in ea*.

127 potiti < *potior*, *-iri* (+ abl.): "to acquire," "get hold of"; *potiti* modifies *mariti* in the preceding verse.

128 Mulier hec: i.e., Belshazzar's wife, the queen. **illi:** i.e., the ideal woman described in vv. 124-7.

129 meretur < *mereor*, *-eri* (dep.): "to deserve," "merit," "be entitled to"; (EL, ML) "to rely on," "be dependent," "be subject to."

130 Eius: "her." **facundia:** "eloquence," "persuasiveness."

131 arguit: < *arguo*, *-ere*: "to prove," "reveal," "betray," "accuse," "charge," "find fault with," "confute."

132 ludendi: cf. *ludus* in v. 1.

133 conceditur < *concedo*, *-ere*: "to allow," "grant," "give." **sollempni** = CL *sollemni* (cf. v. 28).

134 Demus < *do*, *-are*. **huic:** i.e., "the Virgin Mary." **preconia:** CL *praeconia*.

135 concinent < *concino*, *-ere*: "to sing together." **remoti:** "those from afar."

137 Iudee** = CL *Iudeae*.

139, 144, 148 sibi = CL *ei*; in ML *se* is often used for *is* (and, occasionally, vice versa).

139 referamus: see v. 14 and note *ad loc*.

140 prenotavit = LL *praenotavit* < *praenoto*, *-are*: "to warn," "predict."

142 testes: i.e., those who falsely accused Susannah. **comprobavit** < *comprobo*, *-are*: "to prove "x" (acc.) "y" (acc.)."

Babylon hunc exulavit 145
cum Iudeos captivavit,
Balthasar quem honoravit; gaudeamus:
laudes sibi debitas referamus!

Est propheta sanctus Dei:
hunc honorant et Caldei 150
et gentiles et Iudei.
Iubilantes ergo ei, gaudeamus, et cetera.

145-6 These verses refer to the Babylonian Captivity of the Jews. In 597 BCE Nebuchadnezzar besieged Jerusalem and captured the city. He then proceeded to take into exile the king (Jehoiachin) and many leading citizens. Zedekiah was installed as governor of Jerusalem, but when he rebelled, Nebuchadnezzar returned to the city, destroyed the Temple, and deported most of the remaining population to exile in Babylon (586 BCE; cf. 2 *Kings* 24.10-25.21). Some of the Jews returned to Jerusalem by permission of Cyrus, the Persian conqueror of Babylon, in 538 BCE. The entire period from 586-38 was known as the Babylonian Captivity (or the Exile of the Jews) and it dominates much of the Old Testament (cf., e.g., *Psalm* 137.1, *Isaiah* 14.4).

150 Caldei: here the people are meant, not "astrologers" as in v. 47 above.

151 gentiles: (EL) "pagans," "heathens."

ACT II

SCENE 1

Statim apparebit Darius Rex cum principibus suis, 152a
venientque ante eum cythariste et musici sui, psallentes
hec:

Ecce Rex Darius venit cum principibus,
nobilis nobilibus,
Eius et curia resonat leticia, 155
adsunt et tripudia!

Hic est mirandus, cunctis venerandus,
illi imperia sunt tributaria:

SCENE 1 (152a-170)

This brief scene consists entirely of an acclamation of king Darius as he marches upon Babylon. Structurally this mirrors the song of praise sung by the court in honor of Belshazzar (26-45). Like the earlier song, Darius is accorded the highest praise by the chorus of his noblemen who dance (156, 165) and play musical instruments (167-8) in their attempt to create a festive mood of joyous celebration. His defining characteristic seems to be his "nobility" (154, 163, 164). And yet this song reflects the one that was sung to Belshazzar in several other, more negative ways as well. First, a similar note of impiety is struck by Darius' courtiers when they state that their king must be "reverenced" by all (157) and that all "worship" him (159).[56] Also rather disturbing is the fear Darius is said to generate not only among the recently conquered Babylonians, but even his own people (160-2). The mime that concludes the scene brings all these troublesome aspects of Darius' personality vividly to life, as first Belshazzar is killed and then Darius is described sitting on his throne "in majesty" (169a), a final, ominous echo of the earlier song of praise to Belshazzar.[57]

152a Darius: Darius the Mede is mentioned in *Daniel* (e.g., 5.31) as ruling after Belshazzar and before Cyrus, but there exists no other evidence for such a monarch outside of that text. The author of *Daniel* may be thinking of the later Darius I, King of Persia (522-486 BCE), who was the ruler that confirmed the edict permitting the rebuilding of the Temple in 520-515 BCE (*Ezra* 5 and 6). This historical Darius was most famous (at least in Europe) for the defeat of his troops at the hands of the Athenians at Marathon in 490 BCE. **Cythariste** = CL *citharistae* (and see v. 29 and note *ad loc.*).

154 nobilis nobilibus = *nobilis <cum> nobilibus*.

156 tripudia: "dances" (normally performed in religious ceremonies).

157 venerandus = *venerandus <est>*; in CL *veneror* is dep.; in EL/ML the form *venero* occurs in addition to *veneror*.

---

[56] For *adoro*, see vv. 43, 45 and note *ad loc*. The verb *venero* (CL = *veneror*, dep.) occurs in this play at v. 263, where it is used by Darius in his tearful conversation with the condemned Daniel when the king asks him whether he thinks his God, whom he [Daniel] reverences, will save him from death.

[57] For *maiestas*, see vv. 43, 45 and note *ad loc.*; especially significant is the verbal parallel of the phrase *sedente Dario Rege in maiestate sua* (169a) to *Matthew* 19.28, *in sede maiestatis*, 25.31, *in maiestate sua*, and *Luke* 9.26, *in maiestate sua*. Emmerson (1996, 49) states that, "the play does not condemn secular power as intrinsically evil and . . . does not demonize the royal figures. . . . In representing Balthasar and Darius, the play does not caricature or denigrate them. Nor does it show disrespect for the monarchy or question the role of secular authority." Such a view needs to be reconsidered. The playwright's satirical mockery and condemnation of the monarchy is not always blatant (for an exception, cf. v. 225's *O hez*! and note *ad loc.*), but it is pervasive: cf., e.g., the negative depiction of Belshazzar's character in vv. 22-5 and note *ad loc.*; the equation of Belshazzar and God in vv. 43, 45 and note *ad loc.*; a (literal) demonization of Belshazzar's father (v. 107 and note *ad loc*) that is, according to Daniel himself (112-13), equally applicable to the son. One might argue that despite this mountain of evidence, Darius does finally see the light at the end of the play. And yet before that happens he is caricatured far more strongly than his biblical counterpart as a king who, drunk on his own megalomaniacal power, can be easily duped into passing blasphemous legislation that makes the proscription of the original text seem like mild narcissism (cf. vv. 212-23 and note *ad loc.* and Darius' reaction at vv. 224-5 and notes *ad loc.*). In fact, the examples cited above that strongly caricature, criticize, and condemn the institution of monarchy and the individual rulers themselves are either non-existent in the Old Testament narrative or only barely hinted at.

Regem honorant omnes et adorant,
illum Babylonia metuit et patria. 160

Cum armato agmine ruens et cum turbine,
sternit cohortes. confregit et fortes.

Illum honestas colit et nobilitas.
Hic est babylonius nobilis Rex Darius!

Illi cum tripudio gaudeat hec contio, 165
laudet et cum gaudio eius facta fortia tam admirabilia!

Simul omnes gratulemur, resonent et tympana,
cythariste tangant cordas, musicorum organa
resonent ad eius preconia!

Antequam perveniat Rex ad solium suum, 169a
duo precurrentes expellent Balthasar quasi
interficientes eum. Tunc sedente Dario Rege
in maiestate sua, Curia exclamabit:

Rex, in eternum vive! 170

SCENE 2

Tunc duo, flexis genibus, secreto dicent Regi ut 170a
faciat accersiri Danielem. Et Rex iubeat eum
adduci. Illi autem, alius precipientes, dicent hec:

Audite, principes regalis curie,
qui leges regitis tocius patrie:
Est quidam sapiens in Babylonia
secreta reserans deorum gratia.
Eius consilium Regi complacuit, 175
nam prius Balthasar scriptum aperuit.
Ite velociter, ne sit dilatio:
nos uti volumus eius consilio.
Fiat, si venerit, consiliarius
Regis, et fuerit in regno tercius. 180

161 cum turbine: a phrase used in the Old Testament (with *in* instead of *cum*) to describe God's wrath in *Job* 9.17: *in turbine enim conteret me* ("For He [God] crushes me with a whirlwind") and *Isaiah* 30.30: *et auditam faciet Dominus gloriam vocis suae et terrorem brachii sui ostendet in comminatione furoris et flamma ignis devorantis adlidet in turbine et in lapide grandinis* ("And the Lord will cause his majestic voice to be heard and the descending blow of his arm to be seen, in furious anger and a flame of devouring fire, with a cloudburst and whirlwind and hailstones"). Cf. also the Psalmist's wish for God's vengeance to strike his foes (*Psalm* 82.16 in the Vulgate = *Psalm* 83.15): *sic persequere eos in tempestate tua et in turbine* ("in such a way pursue them with your storm and your whirlwind"). Other, similar examples include *Amos* 1.14, *Nahum* 1.3, and *Zechariah* 9.14. Once again the king is equated with God.

165 Illi . . . gaudeat: in CL *gaudeo, -ere* ("to delight in," "show joy in") often takes an abl.; in ML it may also take the dat.

167 gratulemur < *gratulor, -ari*: "to rejoice." **tympana** < *tympanum, -i*: "drum," "tambourine."

168 cythariste* = CL *citharistae*. **cordas** = LL (from the Greek) *chordas* < *chorda, -ae*: "string." **musicorum organa:** according to Dronke (1994, 145), "these could be portable organs or – less specifically – instruments or songs."

169a duo = *duo* <*viri*>. **precurrentes** = CL *praecurrentes*.

Scene 2 (170a-210)

This scene is a significant expansion of its source material, *Daniel* 6.2-4, which relates that after being one of Darius' three principal satraps, Daniel was appointed grand vizier by the king. From this pinnacle Daniel's jealous fellow officials sought to topple him, using religion as their lever. Our playwright begins his scene with the envious nobles secretly persuading Darius to have Daniel brought to court (170a). Instead of doing this themselves, however, they send legates to go and seek him (171-80). After finding Daniel, the legates sing the praises of his "upright character," "subtlety" and "wisdom" (181-92). Daniel's terse reply (four monosyllables) is in Old French, the last time he employs the vernacular in the drama. This seems to reflect, as Dronke 1994, 113-14 suggests, "that with all his fame, he has retained his candid simplicity – his native way of speaking." In the *conductus* (194-206) that the chorus sings as they bring Daniel to the king the actors once again break the dramatic frame of the play and reenter the Christmas celebrations of the present. And unlike the subtle parallel developed between Daniel and Christ in the second *conductus* (136-52), this song contains the play's most sustained and explicit merging of Daniel with Christ.

170a flexis genibus: "on bent knees," i.e., "kneeling." **accersiri** < *accerso, -ere*: "to call," "summon," "bring." **precipientes** = CL *praecipientes* < *praecipio, -ere*: "to instruct."

171 curie* = CL *curiae*; see v. 86 and note *ad loc.* **tocius patrie** = CL *totius patriae*.

174 reserans < *resero, -are*: "to unlock." **gratia:** (abl.) "by the grace of."

176 Balthasar: (gen.)

177 ne sit dilatio: cf. v. 72.

180 tercius = CL *tertius*: "third <most important person>" (presumably after the King and Queen). Cf. also *Daniel* 5.7 (at note to vv. 47-52) and *Daniel* 5.16 (at note to vv. 102-4).

180a ex parte Regis: "on the King's behalf."

Legati, invento Daniele, dicent hec ex parte Regis: 180a

Ex regali venit imperio,
serve Dei, nostra legatio.
Tua Regi laudatur probitas,
te commendat mira calliditas,
Per te solum cum nobis patuit 185
signum dextre, quod omnes latuit.
Te Rex vocat ad suam curiam,
ut agnoscat tuam prudentiam.
Eris supra, ut dicit Darius,
Principalis consiliarius. 190
Ergo veni: iam omnis curia
preparatur ad tua gaudia.

Et Daniel:

G'en vois al Roi.

Conductus Danielis:

Congaudentes celebremus natalis sollempnia:
iam de morte nos redemit Dei Sapientia. 195
Homo natus est in carne, qui creavit omnia,
nasciturum quem predixit prophete facundia
Danielis. Iam cessavit unctionis copia,
cessat regni Iudeorum contumax potentia.
In hoc natalitio, Daniel, cum gaudio te laudat hec contio. 200

181 Ex regali . . . imperio: "under royal authority."

186 dextre* = CL *dextrae*. **quod omnes latuit:** cf. v. 78 and note *ad loc*.

189 supra: "in addition."

192 ad tua gaudia: "for the purpose of <doing> your pleasure," i.e., as Dronke translates it, "so as to do your pleasure."

193 *G'en vois al Roi* = OF "I'll go to the King."

194-206 Dronke's discussion (1994, 114) of this *conductus* is lucid and informative: "The biblical text which made Daniel appear a prophet of Christ was an obscure passage (9, 24-6) about the destruction of Jerusalem, which in the Vetus Latina said that "anointing will be destroyed" (*exterminabitur unctio*) when the "holy one of holy ones" (*sanctus sanctorum* – cf. 273 of our play) will be anointed. . . . Thus as the scholars – alias courtiers – exult in the Christmas festivities, they see Daniel as having proclaimed not only Christ but a new covenant, which supplants the *unctio* and sacral power of Judaism (196-200). From this they pass to the exploits by which Daniel prefigured Christ (201-5) – as saviour of the oppressed (Susannah), as slayer of the dragon, and as himself miraculously delivered from death."

194 congaudentes (EL) < *congaudeo*, *-ere*: "to rejoice with another (person)"; "to rejoice greatly." **celebremus** < *celebro*, *-are*: "to celebrate."

195 redemit < *redimo*, *-ere*: "to redeem," "ransom," "set free."

196 Homo natus est in carne: cf. *John* 1.14: *et Verbum caro factum est* ("and the Word was made flesh").

197 nasciturum . . . facundia = *quem facundia prophete predixit <esse> nasciturum*. **prophete** = LL (from the Greek) *prophetae* < *propheta*, *-ae*: "prophet" (i.e., Daniel; for the prophecy, cf. *Daniel* 9.24-6, cited at n. 12 above).

198 unctionis < *unctio*, *-ionis*: "anointing."

199 contumax: (adj.) "stubborn," "defiant."

200 natalitio = LL *natalicio* < *natalicium*, *-i*: "festive day," "birth."

Tu Susannam liberasti de mortali crimine
cum te Deus inspiravit suo sancto flamine:
Testes falsos comprobasti reos accusamine,
Bel draconem peremisti coram plebis agmine,
Et te Deus observavit leonum voragine— 205
ergo sit laus Dei Verbo genito de virgine!

Et Daniel Regi:

Rex, in eternum vive!

Cui Rex:

Quia novi te callidum, totius regni providum,
te, Daniel, constituo et summum locum tribuo.

Et Daniel Regi:

Rex, michi si credideris, per me nil mali feceris. 210

201 liberasti = (syncopated form of) *liberavisti*. **crimine** < *crimen*, *-inis*: "accusation," "charge."

203 Testes falsos comprobasti: cf. v. 142 above and note *ad loc.*; *comprobasti* is a syncopated form of *comprobavisti*. **accusamine** = CL *accusatione*; *accusamine* seems to be the playwright's own coinage for the sake of his rhyme-scheme.

204-5: *Bel* was another name for Marduk, the chief god of Babylon. The story of Daniel's slaying of the snake (*draconem*) is found only in the Greek translation of *Daniel* made *c.* 100 BCE and later Latin translations of the Greek. The story tells how Daniel destroyed the snake worshipped by the Babylonians as a god – although, as Dentan (1993, 77) notes, "there is no evidence from antiquity that the worship of snakes was ever a feature of Babylonian religion." Daniel then feeds the snake a mixture of pitch, fat, and hair that causes the creature to explode. The king, under pressure from the snake's devoted worshippers, has Daniel thrown into a lions' pit for six days (a doublet taken from *Daniel* 6). While there he is fed by the prophet Habakkuk, airlifted by an angel from Judea for exactly this purpose. On the seventh day an unharmed Daniel is released by the king, who immediately confesses that there is no god but the God of Daniel. Christians viewed Daniel's release from the lions' pit as a foreshadowing of Christ's harrowing of Hell.

204 Bel: (indecl. noun; here = acc.). **peremisti** < *perimo*, *-ere*: "to destroy," "slay," "kill." **coram plebis agmine** = *coram agmine plebis*.

205 voragine = <*in*> *voragine*.

206 Dei Verbo: the "Word of God" = "Christ"; cf. *John* 1.1: *in principio erat Verbum et Verbum erat apud Deum et Deus erat Verbum* ("In the beginning was the Word and the Word was with God and God was the Word").

210 si credideris . . . feceris: (fut. more vivid condition); for the sake of the rhyme scheme, the playwright has substituted *feceris* (fut. perf.) for the more grammatically correct *facies* (fut.).

SCENE 3

Tunc Rex faciet eum sedere iuxta se; et alii consiliarii, Danieli invidentes quia gratior erit Regi, aliis in consilium ductis ut Danielem interficiant, dicent Regi: 210a

Rex, in eternum vive!

Item:

Decreverunt in tua curia
principandi quibus est gloria
Ut ad tui rigorem nominis,
omni spreto vigore numinis, 215
Per triginta dierum spatium
adoreris ut deus omnium, *o Rex!*

Si quis ausu tam temerario
renuerit tuo consilio,
Ut preter te colatur deitas, 220
iudicii sit talis firmitas:
In leonum tradatur foveam—
sic dicatur per totam regiam, *o Rex!*

Et Rex dicat:

Ego mando et remando
ne sit spretum hoc decretum. *O hez!* 225

SCENE 3 (210a-251)

Scene 3 is the dramatic climax of the play. It begins with a short choral song (211-23) – the last in the drama – that recounts the deceitful ploy concocted by the Satraps in *Daniel* 6.7 to trap the king into condemning Daniel to the lions. In the original story the Satraps persuade the king to forbid all of his citizens from addressing "any petition to any god or man" other than Darius himself for one month. The Beauvais playwright substitutes complete idolatry for the somewhat more benign Old Testament proscription, for in the play the king will be worshipped "as God of all" (217) for thirty days. This scheme, then, is the culmination of the views promoting the king's deification previously espoused by the courts of both Belshazzar (26-45) and Darius (153-170a). The king, drunk on the idea of his own divinity, commands the impious legislation to be enacted (224-5). The scene that follows (225a-37), where Daniel is caught praying to his God and the king is forced by his courtiers to sacrifice him on legal grounds, parallels the biblical text closely. What is new is Daniel's heartfelt song (238-45) in which he laments his fate and appeals to the king for mercy.

210a gratior erit Regi: literally, "he will be too agreeable to the King"; or, as Dronke paraphrases it, "he is too much favored by the King." **aliis in consilium ductis:** (abl. abs.).

213 principandi (LL) < *principo, -are*: "to rule."

214 ad tui rigorem nominis: "for the strength of your name," i.e., "in order to reflect the strength of your authority."

215 spreto < *sperno, -ere*: "to remove," "scorn," "reject."

216 Per triginta dierum spatium = *Per spatium triginta dierum*; in CL, duration of time is expressed by the accusative case. In ML, either the ablative could be employed or *per* + acc. **triginta:** (undecl. adj.).

217 adoreris: (2nd sing. pres. pass. subj.).

217 (and 223) o Rex!: this shout is probably an extra-metrical acclamation.

218 temerario: (adj.) "rash," "thoughtless," "foolhardy."

220 preter = CL *praeter*. **deitas:** (EL; nom. sing).

222 In . . . foveam = *tradatur in foveam leonum*.

224 This verse is an echo of Isaiah's caricature of false prophets (*Isaiah* 28.10, 13; only v. 10 is cited here): *quia manda remanda manda remanda expecta reexpecta expecta reexpecta modicum ibi modicum ibi*. ("For command, command again, command, command again, expect, expect again, expect, expect again, a little there, a little here.") **remando:** (EL).

225 O hez!: Darius' utterance is the last vernacular expression in the play. The phrase echoes his courtiers' extra-metrical acclamations of *o Rex*! (217, 223) in the preceding song, but the effect here is comical. Dronke (1994, 145) notes that, "in Old French the exclamation *hez*! is used to urge animals forward [and] is addressed *to* an animal." In particular, it was the cry uttered to urge forward the ass who was led into the church and praised on Jan. 14 during the Feast of the Ass (a close-relative of The Feast of Fools, held on Jan. 1; see **Appendix A** for more on these Feasts and their relationship to the play). A rough equivalent today would be a child uttering "giddy-up." By depicting Darius as inept in his attempt to address his court in the vernacular, the playwright reveals the king to be nothing more than a fallible and foolish human being at the very moment when his court has deified him.

Daniel, hoc audiens, ibit in domum suam et adorabit deum suum; quem emuli videntes, accurrent et dicent Regi: 225a

Nunquid, Dari, observari statuisti omnibus
qui orare vel rogare quicquam a numinibus
ni te deum, illum reum daremus leonibus?
Hoc edictum sic indictum fuit a principibus.

Et Rex, nesciens quare hoc dicerent, respondet:

Vere iussi me omnibus adorari a gentibus. 230

Tunc illi, adducentes Danielem, dicent Regi:

Hunc Iudeum suum deum Danielem vidimus
adorantem et precantem, tuis spretis legibus.

Rex, volens liberare Danielem, dicet:

Nunquam vobis concedatur quod vir sanctus sic perdatur.

Satrape, hoc audientes, ostendent ei legem, dicentes:

Lex Parthorum et Medorum iubet in annalibus
ut qui sprevit que decrevit Rex, detur leonibus. 235

Rex, hoc audiens, velit nolit dicet: 235a

Si sprevit legem quam statueram,
det penas ipse quas decreveram.

225a in domum = CL *domum*. **emuli** = CL *aemuli*: "enemies."

226-30 Cf. *Daniel* 6.13: *tunc respondentes dixerunt coram rege: Daniel de filiis captivitatis Iuda, non curavit de lege tua, et de edicto, quod constituisti: sed tribus temporibus per diem orat obsecratione sua*. ("Then those in response said before the king: "Daniel, who is from the sons of the captivity of Judah, had no regard for your law and the command that you had decreed: but three times each day he prays with his own entreaty.")

226 Nunquid: (interrogative adv.); in CL usually spelled *numquid*.

227 qui orare vel rogare: "who <want> to pray or to request."

228 ni = CL *nisi*

231-2 Note alliteration of "m" (especially "um" and "em") and "s".

234 Parthorum: by 130 BCE the Parthian state extended from the Euphrates to the Indus river. While no historically significant Parthians marked the period in which the story of Daniel is set (*c*. 600-575 BCE), they occupied the same homeland as the Persians and had an empire almost as great in size as their Iranian predecessors. Thus they became identified with the Persians. **Medorum:** a people who rose to power in the Near East and captured the Assyrian capital Nineveh in 612 BCE. Conquered by Cyrus, they became part of the Persian Empire in 549 BCE. During the Babylonian Captivity (see note to vv. 145-6 above) they were expected by Jeremiah (51.11) to be God's instrument for punishing Babylon. *Daniel* 5.31 and 11.1 suppose that the Medes fulfilled this prophecy before the rise of the Persians, which is unhistorical. In the ancient and medieval worlds "Medes" was synonymous with "Persians." **annalibus:** < (adj.) *annalis*, *-e*: (masc. pl. as substantive) "annals," "chronicles," "records."

235a-7 These lines reflect some of the most interesting social, legal, and religious questions that the cathedral schools were exploring in the twelfth century. Darius, the recently self-created all-powerful divinity, cannot change his own law. Is this because Darius perceives "law" to be greater than divinity? Does Darius fear that by disobeying his own law he will appear to his subjects as a false god and thus lose his (divine?) right to rule? What is the exact relationship between secular and divine law or, more generally speaking, between the state and religion?

235a velit nolit: "willing or not," "by compulsion."

237 det penas: *poenas dare* is an idiom that means "to pay the penalty." **penas** = CL *poenas*.

Tunc satrape rapient Danielem, et ille, respiciens Regem, dicet:

Heu, heu, heu! quo casu sortis
venit hec dampnatio mortis?
Heu, heu, heu!—scelus infandum!— 240
cur me dabit ad lacerandum

hec fera turba feris?
Sic me, Rex, perdere queris?
Heu, qua morte mori
me cogis? Parce furori! 245

Et Rex, non valens eum liberare, dicet ei:

Deus quem colis tam fideliter
te liberabit mirabiliter.

Tunc proicient Danielem in lacum, statimque angelus, tenens gladium, comminabitur leonibus ne tangant eum. Et Daniel, intrans lacum, dicet: 247a

Huius rei non sum reus:
miserere mei, Deus— *eleyson!*

Mitte, Deus, huc patronum 250
qui refrenet vim leonum— *eleyson!*

238-45 This unadorned speech (almost prosaic in its minimal use of rhetorical dress and simple meter) renders Daniel's shock and horror at his impending doom by means of repeated *heu* (238, 240, and 244) and short – often elliptical – phrases and questions. The music that accompanies the lyrics allows the freest rein in the play to emotional expression and is the greatest departure from traditional liturgical forms (such as Gregorian chant) in the score.

239 dampnatio = CL *damnatio*.

242 fera . . . feris: the wordplay suggestively links the behavior of the crowd with the lions.

243 Sic me, Rex, perdere queris: cf. *Luke* 19.47: *et erat docens cotidie in templo principes autem sacerdotum et scribae et principes plebis quaerebant illum perdere*. ("And he [Jesus] was teaching daily in the temple. The chief priests and the scribes and the principal men of the people sought to destroy him.") **queris*** = CL *quaeris*.

245a non valens: "powerless."

246-7 Cf. *Daniel* 6.16: *tunc rex praecepit: et adduxerunt Danielem, et miserunt eum in lacum leonum. Dixitque rex Danieli: Deus tuus, quem colis semper, ipse liberabit te*. ("Then the king made his command, and they led Daniel out and cast him into the lions' pit. And the king said to Daniel: "Your God, whom you always worship, will himself free you."")

247a lacum < *lacus*, *-us*: "pit." **comminabitur** < *comminor*, *-ari* (+ dat.): "to threaten violently."

249 miserere mei, Deus: Daniel here utters a common quote from the *Psalms* (4.2, 50.3, 55.2, 56.2).

249, 251 eleyson!: (EL from the Greek) "have mercy!"; this word is taken from the liturgical invocation *Kyrie, eleyson* ("Lord, have mercy!") that precedes the Gloria in the Roman Catholic and Eastern Orthodox Masses.

SCENE 4

Interea alius angelus admonebit Abacuc prophetam ut deferat prandium quod portabat messoribus suis Danieli in lacum leonum, dicens: 251a

Abacuc, tu senex pie, ad lacum Babylonie
Danieli fer prandium: mandat tibi Rex omnium.

Cui Abacuc:

Novit Dei cognitio quod Babylonem nescio,
neque lacus est cognitus quo Daniel est positus. 255

SCENE 4 (251a-272)

In this scene the playwright grafts onto the pit narrative from *Daniel* 6.17-23 an episode from its doublet in *Daniel* 14.32-8, where a later ruler, Cyrus, condemns Daniel for a second time to the lion-pit (for the details, see note to vv. 204-5). This episode told how an angel brought the prophet Habakkuk from Judea to Babylon to provide Daniel with food. The scene closes with the king sending the scheming courtiers to their deaths. Unlike his source (*Daniel* 6.24), however, our writer spares the courtiers' wives and children from also being thrown to the lions. Also of note is an addition to the original story of a scene in which the condemned officials, at the moment before their death, stand stripped of their clothes at the pit-edge and admit their guilt and repent (268-70).

251a-61a Cf. *Daniel* 14.32-8: *erat autem Habacuc propheta in Iudaea, et ipse coxerat pulmentum, et intriverat panes in alveolo: et ibat in campum ut ferret messoribus.* 33 *dixitque Angelus Domini ad Habacuc: fer prandium, quod habes, in Babylonem Danieli, qui est in lacu leonum.* 34 *et dixit Habacuc: Domine, Babylonem non vidi, et lacum nescio.* 35 *et apprehendit eum Angelus Domini in vertice eius, et portavit eum capillo capitis sui, posuitque eum in Babylone supra lacum in impetu spiritus sui.* 36 *et clamavit Habacuc, dicens: Daniel serve Dei, tolle prandium, quod misit tibi Deus.* 37 *et ait Daniel: recordatus es mei Deus, et non dereliquisti diligentes te.* 38 *surgensque Daniel comedit. porro Angelus Domini restituit Habacuc confestim in loco suo.* ("Now there was in Judea a prophet called Habakkuk, and he himself had cooked some food, and had broken bread in a tray, and was going into the field to bring it to the harvesters. 33 And the Angel of the Lord said to Habakkuk, "Bring the meal which you have to Babylon for Daniel, who is in a lions' pit." 34 And Habakkuk said: "Lord, I have not seen Babylon and I do not know this pit." 35 And the Angel of the Lord took him by the top of his head and carried him by the hair of his head and placed him in Babylon above the pit in the force of his spirit. 36 And Habakkuk cried out, saying, "Daniel, servant of God, take the meal which God has sent to you." 37 And Daniel said: "You have remembered me, O God, and you have not abandoned those that love you." 38 And Daniel got up and ate. In addition, the Angel of the Lord restored Habakkuk at once to his own land.")

251a Abacuc: Habakkuk was a little known prophet in Judah at the end of the seventh century BCE. The Old Testament book bearing his name was composed between 609-598 BCE when the Babylonian armies under Nebuchadnezzar invaded Palestine.

251a messoribus < *messor, -oris*: "harvester," "reaper."

252 Babylonie = CL *Babyloniae*.

253 mandat tibi Rex omnium: cf. Darius' words at v. 224 (*Ego mando et remando*) and the deification of Darius by the scheming counselors at v. 217 (*ut deus omnium*).

254-5 These verses expand slightly on Habakkuk's terse reply to the angel in the original (*Daniel* 14.34, *Domine, Babylonem non vidi, et lacum nescio*). In the play, Habakkuk bluntly states that God should know that he, Habakkuk, is ignorant of such things. Note too the antithesis of the first and last words of v. 254 (*Novit . . . nescio*) and the repetition of *cognitio . . . cognitus* in the same metrical position. The playwright allows Habakkuk some wittily constructed lines in a rather awkward moment.

255 lacus est cognitus = *lacus est cognitus* <*mihi*>.

Tunc angelus, apprehendens eum capillo capitis sui, ducet ad lacum. Et Abacuc, Danieli offerens prandiun, dicet: 255a

Surge, frater, ut cibum capias:
tuas Deus vidit angustias;
Deus misit—da Deo gratias
qui te fecit.

El Daniel, cibum accipiens, dicet:

Recordatus es mei, domine! 260
Accipiam in tuo nomine—alleluia!

His transactis, angelus reducet Abacuc in locum suum. Tunc Rex, descendens de solio suo, veniet ad lacum, dicens lacrimabiliter: 261a

Tene, putas, Daniel, salvabit ut eripiaris
a nece proposita, quem tu colis et veneraris?

Et Daniel Regi:

Rex, in eternum vive!

Item:

Angelicum solita misit pietate patronum,
quo Deus ad tempus conpescuit ora leonum.

Tunc Rex gaudens exclamabit:

Danielem educite et emulos immittite!

Cum expoliati fuerint et venerint ante lacum, clamabunt: 267a

Merito hec patimur, quia peccavimus:
in sanctum Dei iniuste egimus,
iniquitatem fecimus! 270

257-8 Deus . . . Deus . . . Deo: note Habakkuk's triple repetition of *Deus*.

257 angustias < *angustia*, *-ae*: (sing. very rare) "difficulty," "distress," "anxiety."

258 Deus misit: an ellipitical phrase that can mean "God has sent me," "God has sent this help/salvation," or "God has sent this food" (as per *Daniel* 14.36). The object of the verb is of no importance since the idea that God has sent something is alone sufficient to alleviate Daniel's distress.

261 Accipiam: Daniel's response, like Habakkuk's laconic phrase in 258 (*Deus misit*), also omits its object. The two ellipses rhetorically underline the theological point that whatever God sends one must accept. **alleluia!:** "Hallelujah" is Hebrew and means "Praise the Lord!"

261a-6 Cf. *Daniel* 6.20-22: *appropinquansque lacui, Danielem voce lacrimabili inclamavit, et affatus est eum*: *Daniel serve Dei viventis, Deus tuus, cui tu servis semper, putasne valuit te liberare a leonibus*? 21 *et Daniel regi respondens ait*: *Rex, in aeternum vive*! 22 *Deus meus misit angelum suum, et conclusit ora leonum, et non nocuerunt mihi: quia coram eo iustitia inventa est in me*: *sed et coram te, rex, delictum non feci*. ("And drawing near to the pit, he [Darius] cried out to Daniel in a tearful voice, and said to him, "Daniel, servant of the living God, do you think your God, whom you always serve, has been able to free you from the lions?" 21 And Daniel in response to the king said, "King, live for ever! 22 My god has sent his angel and has shut up the mouths of the lions and they have not harmed me. For before God justice has been found in me. But before you, O king, I have done no wrong."")

262 Tene: *Te* + *ne*. **salvabit:** (EL) < *salvo*, *-are*: "to save," "heal," "be saved."

263 nece < *nex*, *necis*: "death."

265 Angelicum . . . patronum: note the chiastic word order (abcba). **solita . . . pietate:** (abl. abs.).

266 ad tempus: "for the time," "for a short time." **conpescuit** = CL *compescuit*.

267 emulos* = CL *aemulos*.

267a expoliati: (ML) "stripped."

270 iniquitatem < *iniquitas*, *-atis*: "shameful deed," "unfair act."

Illi, proiecti in lacum, statim consumentur a leonibus. 270a
Et Rex, videns hoc, dicet:

Deum Danielis qui regnat in seculis
adorari iubeo a cunctis populis!

CONCLUSION

Daniel, in pristinum gradum receptus, prophetabit: 272a

Ecce venit sanctus ille, sanctorum sanctissimus,
quem rex iste iubet coli potens et fortissimus.
Cessant phana, cesset regnum, cessabit et unctio: 275
instat regni Iudeorum finis et oppressio.

Tunc angelus ex inproviso exclamabit: 276a

Nuntium vobis fero de supernis:
natus est Christus, dominator orbis,
in Bethleem Iude—sic enim propheta
dixerat ante. 280

His auditis, cantores incipient Te Deum Laudamus. 280a

Finit Daniel.

271-2 Cf. *Daniel* 6.26: *a me constitutum est decretum, ut in universo imperio et regno meo, tremiscant et paveant Deum Danielis: ipse est enim Deus vivens, et aeternus in saecula, et regnum eius non dissipabitur, et potestas eius usque in aeternum.* ("I have established a decree, that in all my royal dominion men tremble and fear before the God of Daniel, for he is the living God, enduring for ever; his kingdom will not be destroyed, and his power will continue forever.")

271 seculis = CL *saeculis*.

CONCLUSION (272a-280a)

Daniel moves from the role of sage and devout Jew to prophet foretelling the coming of Christ and, consequently, the end of the Jewish kingdom. The prophecy is immediately fulfilled as an angel announces that the Christ child is born in Bethlehem. The entire cast (and very likely some of the audience) responds by singing the *Te Deum*.

272a pristinum gradum: "former rank." **prophetabit:** (EL from the Greek) < *propheto, -are*: "to prophesy."

273 sanctus . . . sanctorum sanctissimus: cf. *Daniel* 9.24 (cited at n. 12 above).

275 Cessant . . . cesset . . . cessabit: the sequence of tenses and moods is quite peculiar (pres. indic.; pres. subj.; fut. indic.), but, as Dronke (1994, 146) believes, "the pres. indic. and subj. probably have future force here." Otherwise, translate (somewhat awkwardly) as: "cease . . . must cease . . . will cease." **phana** = CL *fana* < *fanum, -i*: "temple."

276 oppressio < *oppressio, -onis*: "overthrow."

277a inproviso (adv.) = CL *improviso*: "unexpectedly," "suddenly."

277-80 The angel's song, whose words are from a famous older lyric by Fulbert of Chartres, are sung to the only completely liturgical music in the play, a celebrated eleventh-century hymn.

277-9 Cf. the Angel to the shepherds in Luke 2.11: *quia natus est vobis hodie salvator qui est Christus Dominus in civitate David.* ("For today in the city of David is born to you a savior, who is Christ the Lord.")

279 Iude = CL *Iudae*. **propheta*:** (EL; cf. v. 197).

280a Te Deum Laudamus: the *Te Deum*, with its repetitive melodic line, is the great celebratory hymn of the Medieval Latin church. Dating from the third-century, it was sung after the ninth responsory at Matins (the midnight vigil), at the end of High Mass on feast days, and at other celebrations, including the end of many plays. Together with the angel's song that preceded it, the *Te Deum* signals a return from the world of the play and reintegration with the life of the contemporary church. The congregation of audience-worshippers may have sung along with the cast either in Latin or in the vernacular.

Ordo Virtutum

("The Play of the Virtues")

c. 1152

HILDEGARD OF BINGEN

"Hildegard." *Nuremberg Chronicle*, fol. CCIv.

Introduction

1 Hildegard of Bingen (1098-1179)

H(ildegard) of Bingen, a German nun, writer, and composer, was born in 1098 of noble parents. At the age of eight she was sent to a convent run by an abbess named Jutta, where, despite being a sickly child prone to visions (perhaps a result of migraines or epilepsy[58]), she was given a rudimentary education in Latin, the scriptures, and music. H. became a nun, and at the death of Jutta in 1136, succeeded her as abbess. Soon thereafter she achieved immediate fame from her visions and her writings, and was acclaimed by bishops and the Pope.[59] Unfortunately, her increasing celebrity left her little time to pursue her religious studies and devotions. It was probably for these reasons that in 1150 she founded a new convent in Rupertsberg near the town of Bingen.

At Rupertsberg H. taught theology and medicine, writing an encyclopedia, the *Physica*, on the pharmaceutical properties of herbs, trees, and gems that was eventually used as a textbook by the Montpellier medical school, the most celebrated in medieval Europe. Among her other important works were *Causae et Curae* ("Causes and Cures"; a medical text on physical and mental diseases that included both theory and remedies) and three major visionary and theological texts: *Scivias* ("Know the Ways <of the Lord>"), *Liber Vitae Meritorum* ("Book of Life's Merits"), and *Liber Divinorum Operum* ("Book of the Divine Works").[60]

In addition to her accomplishments in the fields of theology and medicine, H. also possessed a talent for musical composition. She wrote seventy-seven liturgical songs for her nuns, as well as the music for her play, *Ordo Virtutum*. H. gathered her songs into a lyrical cycle which she called *Symphonia Harmoniae Caelestium Revelationum* ("Symphony of the Harmony of Heavenly Revelations"). As Dronke (1985, 8-9) notes, "*Symphonia* is a key concept in Hildegard's thought, and one that she discusses in early as well as late works. It designates not only a harmony of diverse notes produced by human voices and instruments, but also the celestial harmony within a human being. The human soul, according to Hildegard, is *symphonialis* ("symphonic"), and it is this characteristic that expresses itself both in the inner accord of soul and body and in human music-making. Music is at the same time earthly and heavenly – produced by earthly means, but able to evoke for mankind, at least briefly and partially, the heavenly consonance that they possessed fully in Paradise before the Fall. *Symphonia* implies an exultation of the mind, to which the vocal celebration and the instrumental execution correspond." In recent years H.'s music has been rediscovered and popularized in many recordings.[61]

---

[58] For an investigation of the nature and meaning of H.'s visions, especially with respect to their being caused by migraine headaches, see Flanagan 1989, 193-213.

[59] In 1141 she began to dictate her first literary work, *Scivias*, which contained prophecies authenticated by the Pope.

[60] In addition to these medical and visionary theological texts, H. also wrote hundreds of letters, exegitical works, homilies, saints' lives, and a glossary of a secret language (*Lingua Ignota*).

[61] See **Appendix D** for a list of H.'s music available on compact disc, MP3s, and DVD.

H. died in 1179, and although her earliest biographer proclaimed her a saint and miracles were reported during her life and at her tomb, she has not been formally canonized. She is, however, listed as a saint in the Roman Martyrology and is honored on her feast day (September 17) in certain German dioceses.

2 Visions and Art

(*i*) Visions

H.'s visions, unsurpassed in medieval literature for their graphic detail and mystical expressiveness, had been with her since childhood. In 1175 she described them in a letter to Guibert of Gembloux as emanating from, "the reflection (or "shadow") of the living light" (*umbra viventis luminis*). This reflection was a kind of radiance that, while always in her view, did not block her normal vision. In her experiences of this divine radiance H. claimed to, "see, hear, and know all at once." In addition, she notes that, "the words in this vision are not like words uttered by the mouth of man, but like a shimmering flame, or a cloud floating on a clear day." These visions remained with her throughout her life and sometimes produced painful physical experiences. H. was given assistance in recording her visions by two individuals: Richardis von Stade, a nun to whom she was deeply attached, and a monk named Volmar, a close friend and secretary who often corrected her Latin.

(*ii*) A Multimedia Artist

Like her visions, which mixed images and words, H.'s works (many of them based directly on her visions) exhibit a very close connection between the visual, aural, and verbal. In this respect, H.'s poetic creations are typical of those of the medieval world. But unlike the majority of other artists of this period who specialized in only one area of creative endeavor, the almost unique quality with H. is that she herself was the writer, composer and illustrator (or, at the least, visual designer) of her works. This is especially true of her one drama, the *Ordo Virtutum*, which was written for performance by the nuns of her convent at Bingen.[62]

---

[62] Probably in honor of the official consecration of H.'s new convent in 1152. H. may have also designed the costumes for this performance. We know from her letters that she and her nuns wore costly garments and jewelry during special feast days (see **Appendix C**, letter A) and that in the first visionary work she completed, the *Scivias* (1150), the miniatures that illustrate the text describing the Virtues depict each one with her own special dress and attributes; e.g., Fear of God has a dark dress covered in closed eyes painted in silver, Discipline has a purple garment which protects her from sinful lusts, Victory is armed as a knight, and Humility wears a golden crown and a mirror on her breast in which Christ's image is reflected.

3 *Ordo Virtutum*

(*i*) Poetic Language and Technique

H.'s literary technique, among the most unusual in medieval lyric, is noteworthy for its freedom from conventional metrical forms and its ability to transform different kinds of Latin (biblical, liturgical, and colloquial) into a new type of poetic language.[63] H. achieves this peculiar synthesis in the *Ordo* through a variety of means, including the use of such rhetorical tropes as antithesis (e.g., 21, 66-7, 144, and 248) anaphora (161-3) and wordplay (e.g., 137, 235-7). The most important of all her literary techniques, though, and the one for which she is justly celebrated, is her creative use of metaphor (e.g., 5, 8, 14, 24, 27, etc.). H.'s metaphors are so extensive in the *Ordo*, and of such variety (simple, elaborate, compressed, allusive, etc.), that I have singled them out for special comment in the notes.

Another interesting aspect of H.'s literary technique in the *Ordo* is her use of verbal repetitions (e.g., *umbra* in 8, 12, and 108; *amplector* in 49, 105, 125, 127, 195, and 209). Similar words and phrases are repeated several times in a variety of contexts where ideas can be either reinforced or reconsidered. This use of intratextuality also creates a verbal tapestry that binds the play together structurally and thematically.

In addition, H. is especially fond in the *Ordo* of employing biblical allusion (an example of intertextuality). Indeed, a knowledge of the specific texts that H. reworks for her play is essential to understanding her art. The most important of these have been cited in the notes in Latin, along with English translations. Since a brief introduction to the biblical texts from which H. drew much of her language and many of her theological ideas may be of use to the student, background information to the *Song of Solomon*, *Isaiah*, *John*, and the *Apocalypse* follows.

1. *Song of Solomon* (also called the *Song of Songs*):

The *Song of Solomon* is a short work (it has fewer than two hundred poetic verses) dealing with the sensual love between a man and a woman. It is, perhaps, the most anomalous book in the Bible (e.g., it is the only one in which God is never named). The *Song* was composed orally over a period of centuries before finally being written down sometime in the years between 400-200 BCE. Its intense style of love poetry, which includes lush, extravagant imagery appealing to the senses of smell, taste, and touch, detailed descriptions of the human body (both male and female), and highly stylized terms of endearment such as "dove", "sister" and "king" link the *Song* to the amorous verse of other ancient Near Eastern and Mediterranean cultures (especially those of Egypt, Babylon, and, perhaps, the Classical and Hellenistic Greek worlds). Jews and Christians accepted the *Song* as an authentic text of the Bible largely because the former came to read it as an allegory of

---

[63] Unlike her peers (including the two other playwrights in this edition), H. had no formal learning. Her lack of a scholarly education (which would have consisted primarily of a grounding in logic and patristic writings) can in some ways explain her unusual style. For an appreciation of the literary qualities of H.'s *Ordo* viewed from within the context of Medieval Latin lyric poetry, see Dronke 1970, 178-9 and Iversen 1992.

God's love for Israel and the latter as Christ's love for the Church or for the believing soul.[64] It was the intense descriptions of love in the *Song* – often enhanced by reference to a variety of different flora and fauna – that struck a powerful chord with H. Indeed, in one sense H.'s play is really an extended meditation on the intensity of God's love for the human soul described through the (allegorically and spiritually filtered) imagery taken from the *Song*.

2. *Isaiah*:

This text has played a central role in Christian liturgy and theology. It is sometimes called the "Fifth Gospel" because, in the words of Jerome, Isaiah recounts the life of the Messiah in such a way as to make one think he is "telling the story of what has already happened rather than what is still to come." H. took from *Isaiah* several images and ideas (e.g., "clouds," 1; "Jesse tree motif," 78; "sailing ships," 249; "New Jerusalem," 134, 157, 204, and 251) that function as metaphorical symbols of some of the most important themes in her play.

3. *Gospel of John*:

Unlike the gospels of *Matthew*, *Mark*, and *Luke*, the gospel of *John* presents the life of Jesus from a more intense theological perspective with a special focus on Jesus as Christ and God. In fact, John's portrayal of Jesus as "God on earth" solidified the early Church's view of itself as a "Christ-is-God" centered religion. But it was this gospel's use of repetitive – and at times incantatory – language infused with such mystical metaphors and symbolic portrayals of Christ as the "Word of God" (*John* 1.1ff.; cf. *Ordo* 3), the "fountain of eternal life" (*John* 4.14; cf. *Ordo* 95) and the "Good Shepherd" (*John* 10.11; cf. *Ordo* 169) that particularly appealed to H.

4. *Apocalypse* (also called *Revelation*):

It is no surprise that H. was fascinated by the *Apocalypse*, the final book of the Bible. Indeed, its vivid imagery and cryptic symbols arranged within a kaleidoscope of scenes punctuated by voices and bursts of heavenly hymnody mirror those of H.'s play. Even the plot of H.'s drama replays – though on a more intimate level – that of the *Apocalypse*: in a cosmic war of good versus evil, Satan, at first triumphant, is in the end overthrown and a new age is initiated where all souls live in peace with God.

[64] The most famous medieval example of the allegorical method of reading the *Song* is the eighty-six homilies of H.'s contemporary (and correspondent) St. Bernard of Clairvaux, which cover only the first two chapters.

(*ii*) A Radical Play: Feminism, and Narrative

In the Western European medieval worldview a person's soul was constantly threatened by three powerful enemies: the world, the flesh, and the Devil. Salvation was to be obtained only by sincere and thorough repentance. In addition to the *Ordo Virtutum*, a considerable proportion of medieval literature dwells on such concerns; and it was evidently considered a valid and important function of poetry to stimulate moral reflection and penitential contrition. This traditional aspect of the *Ordo*, representing as it does the culture in which it was created, seems alien to present-day concerns. That the play transcends its cultural world is largely due to two factors:

1. The *Ordo* is a gynocentric text in which H. can be seen as a woman struggling to redefine the meaning of her world theologically and socially from a feminine perspective. The world in which H. lived and worked as an aristocratic nun is well described by Cantor (1993, 355): "In these convents daughters and widows of the aristocracy were cloistered by their families and removed from noble households, sometimes for exalted religious reasons, sometimes to suit the mundane convenience of their families. These aristocratic nuns chafed under severe discipline and control by men, such as the bishop who exercised discipline over them and the priest-confessor who was assigned to take care of their souls." It is within such a culture as this that one must situate H. and understand her works.

2. The stylized presentation of theology in the *Ordo* is remarkably innovative. Instead of borrowing a story from the Bible or one of the legends surrounding a saint's life, as the majority of medieval playwrights did, H. created her own allegorical characters and narrative. Indeed, the real action here is an inventive mix of (often radical) theological ideas and suspense, since the outcome of the story is, unlike those of other plays of H.'s time, unknown to the audience. An accurate description of the narrative might be "The Soul's Journey," which, viewed from a modern perspective, one can read as a reversal of the typical movie plot: here Devil meets girl, Devil gets girl, Devil loses girl. An outline of the narrative follows[65]:

Prologue (1-8).
The Virtues are greeted by the Patriarchs and Prophets.

Scene 1 (9-67).
The Soul comes in innocence, and calls to the Virtues.
The Devil seduces the Soul.

Scene 2 (68-158).
Led by Humility, the Virtues sing of their powers and their solidarity against the Devil.

[65] There are no indications in the manuscripts of scene breaks. Those included in the outline and text were first made by Dronke, who employed them in his edition of the play to indicate the general structure and thematic organization of the narrative.

Scene 3 (159-208).
The Soul returns to the Virtues in penitence, seeking their aid.

Scene 4 (209-51).
The Soul, aided by the Virtues, fights against the Devil and overcomes his powers; Victory is proclaimed.

Conclusion (252-69).
The Soul, Humility and the Virtues are joined by the Patriarchs, Prophets and other Souls imprisoned in the flesh to sing of the joy of steadfastness, and give thanks for God's mercy.

(*iii*) Meter & Music

H. composed words and music to function in unison. Unlike the tightly structured, regular metrical stanzas of the *Tres Clerici* or the use of various accentual and quantitative metres in the *Danielis Ludus*, H.'s poetry is genrally free of traditional metrical structures (in contemporary terms one would call it "free verse" or "poetic prose"). Indeed, there are no stanzas per se, but a free-floating line that both acts upon and reacts to the movement and rhythm of the melody. H.'s musical style has no direct ancestors or descendants.[66]

Despite this extreme metrical freedom, there still exist variations between the rhythmic patterns spoken by various characters. Dronke (1994, 155) observes that, "there is a clear differentiation between the five speeches of *Diabolus* ["the Devil"], which move in a jagged staccato fashion, and the flowing cadences, lyrical and even incantatory in rhythm, which the virtues deploy. *Anima* ["the Soul"], when she is in harmony with the Virtues, does likewise, but at the moment she defies them, her words take on something of *Diabolus*' jaggedness."

There is no music for the Devil's speeches in the manuscript. This is not surprising, since H. considered the ability to make music a divine attribute. The Devil's lines are either spoken or shouted (cf. *strepitus* in the rubric at 47a).

---

[66] For an analysis of the music in the *Ordo*, see Davidson 1992.

Incipit *Ordo Virtutum*

PROLOGUE

Patriarche et Prophete:
Qui sunt hi, qui ut nubes?

Virtutes:
O antiqui sancti, quid admiramini in nobis?
Verbum Dei clarescit in forma hominis,
et ideo fulgemus cum illo,
edificantes membra sui pulcri corporis. 5

Patriarche et Prophete:
Nos sumus radices et vos rami,
fructus viventis oculi,
et nos umbra in illo fuimus.

PROLOGUE (1-8)

The play opens with a concentrated series of images – clouds, the Word made flesh, radiant light, constructing Christ's body, the roots, branches, and fruits of the living eye, and shadow – that present a stylized theological world through allusive, and often bizarre, metaphors whose meanings and importance will only become clear later in the drama.

Patriarche et Prophete = CL *Patriarchae et Prophetae*. It is not surprising that H. begins with a chorus of Old Testament patriarchs and prophets for, as Flanagan (1989, 64) notes, "Hildegard took pains to locate herself within the prophetic tradition of the Old Testament, as the opening formulae of her works indicate."

1 qui ut nubes = *qui <sunt> ut nubes*; cf. *Isaiah* 60.8: *qui sunt isti qui ut nubes volant et quasi columbae ad fenestras suas*? ("Who are these that fly like clouds, and like doves to their windows?"). H.'s allusion to the most important of all Old Testament prophets in v. 1 is more complex than first meets the eye. The Virtues are "like clouds" because they are spiritual beings that are intangible and reside in heaven. But this verse of *Isaiah* is also part of a series of images in chapter 60 of that text that deals with the building of the heavenly Jerusalem – one of the most significant themes in the play (cf. 134, 157, 204, and 251).

1a Virtutes: Newman (1987, 17) points out that each Virtue is, "not a personified moral quality, but a numinous force that appears in human form only because it empowers human action. . . . Like Christ and the Church, the Virtues have a dual nature; they indicate, first, divine grace and, second, human cooperation. Through them Hildegard conveyed her profound conception of synergy – salvation as the joint effort of God and humanity."

3 Verbum Dei . . . hominis: a condensed paraphrase of *John* 1.1-14, especially verses 1: *In principio erat verbum, et verbum erat apud Deum, et Deus erat verbum* ("In the beginning was the word, and the word was with God, and God was the word") and 14: *Et verbum caro factum est, et habitavit in nobis* ("And the word was made flesh, and dwelled in us").

4 fulgemus < *fulgeo, -ere*: "to shine."

5 edificantes = CL *aedificantes* < *aedifico, -are*: "to build up," "construct." **membra:** Christians metaphorically viewed the Church as either the body of Christ or, by extension, as the limbs of Christ's body (*sui pulc<h>ri corporis*).

7 fructus: (nom. pl.). **viventis oculis:** a compressed metaphorical image. The "living eye" is both "the sun" and "God." In addition, Dronke (1994, 148) observes that, "*Oculus*, which means both "eye" and "bud", unifies the imagery of light and growth: the divine sunlight ripens these fruits, that are the culmination of the tree of the Word, whose divine buds burgeon on earth."

8 nos umbra in illo fuimus: H.'s expression refers allusively both to the Patriarchs' and Prophets' (especially Isaiah's) foreshadowing of the coming of Christ and to the image of Christ's towering presence overshadowing his predecessors.

SCENE 1

Querela Animarum in carne positarum:
O nos peregrine sumus.
Quid fecimus, ad peccata deviantes? 10
Filie regis esse debuimus,
sed in umbram peccatorum cecidimus.
O vivens sol, porta nos in humeris tuis
in iustissimam hereditatem quam in Adam perdidimus!
O rex regum, in tuo prelio pugnamus. 15

SCENE 1 (8a-67)

H. quickly establishes a contrast between a group of embodied Souls who lament their flawed existence trapped on the earth in mortal bodies (9-15) and Anima ("Soul"), the play's heroine, who happily foresees the day when she will be restored to heaven in the "radiant robe" of her glorified body (16-19). After praising Anima for "loving much" (20-2), the Virtues announce their willingness to aid her in the battle against sin which all souls on earth must fight (25). Anima at once grows despondent and laments the difficulty of fighting the desires of the flesh (26-8). Although the Virtues (in particular, Knowledge of God) attempt to comfort her, she defies them (29-47). In the midst of this division that has arisen between the Virtues and Anima, the Devil appears. His initial words to Anima do not simply parrot her justification to the Virtues that she only wishes to enjoy the world and not do it any harm, but rephrase it in such a way that equates sexual pleasure with great honor (*amplectetur te magno honore*, 49). Anima is convinced by this argument and at once exits. The Virtues, now bereft of Anima, grieve over her loss and summon Innocence (another Virtue) to mourn with them (50-8). Their song of lamentation also functions to expose the Devil's attempt to conceal in specious language the sins of the flesh (*delectatio carnis*, *lasciviam*). The Devil retorts by mocking Innocence's power (*pudore bono*) before asserting that he can give everything to those who follow him (59-61). He then concludes his speech by mocking Humility's powerlessness as well as that of all the Virtues, claiming that they are ignorant of their own nature (61-2). Humility does not reply to the Devil's taunts but tells him that she knows who he is: the rebel who wanted to surpass God, but instead was hurled into the abyss (63-66). The scene ends with the Virtues drawing a sharp contrast between their present abode and that of the Devil (67).

8a *Querela Animarum in carne positarum* = "The lament (*querela*) of Souls placed in flesh," i.e., "The lament of embodied Souls."

9 peregrine = CL *peregrinae*.

10 deviantes: LL compound of *de* + *vio*, *-are* (a verb created from the noun *via*): "to turn away," "turn away from what is good to what is evil or false."

11 Filie = CL *Filiae*.

12 umbra: contrast the meaning of *umbra* here with that of v. 8.

13 O vivens sol: cf. *viventis oculis* in v. 7. **in humeris tuis:** "on your shoulders." The image is derived from *Luke* 15.5 (the parable of the lost sheep): *et cum invenerit eam, inponit in umeros suos gaudens* ("And when he [the shepherd] has found it, he places it on his shoulders, rejoicing"). For the same image, see also v. 169 and note *ad loc*. Another parallel is found in Book 2 of Vergil's *Aeneid* (perhaps the best known pagan work of literature in the Middle Ages), where Aeneas recounts to Dido his escape from Troy carrying his aged father Anchises on his shoulders (vv. 707ff.).

14 in iustissimam hereditatem: the "most just inheritance" is paradise, which was lost to all souls, according to H., "by Adam." The fact that H. does not mention Eve here is surprising, since most Christian writers (nearly all of whom were male) tended to blame her for mankind's fall from grace and expulsion from the Garden of Eden. Adam, on the other hand, was usually portrayed by medieval theologians as complicit only by association with Eve. **in Adam:** *Adam* is a Hebrew word that is declined in Latin as a first declension noun. *Adam* itself may be either nom. or acc.

15 prelio = CL *proelio*.

Felix Anima:
O dulcis divinitas, et o suavis vita,
in qua perferam vestem preclaram,
illud accipiens quod perdidi in prima apparitione,
ad te suspiro, et omnes Virtutes invoco.

Virtutes:
O felix Anima, et o dulcis creatura Dei, 20
que edificata es in profunda altitudine sapientie Dei,
multum amas.

Felix Anima:
O libenter veniam ad vos,
ut prebeatis michi osculum cordis.

Virtutes:
Nos debemus militare tecum, o filia regis. 25

Sed, gravata, Anima conqueritur:
O gravis labor, et o durum pondus
quod habeo in veste huius vite,
quia nimis grave michi est contra carnem pugnare.

17 perferam: "I will wear." **vestem preclaram** = CL *vestem praeclaram*: "radiant robe"; metaphorical for the kind of existence Anima will have in heaven where her human body will be spiritually transformed.[67] Throughout this scene H. makes explicit her view (and that of the Catholic Church) that human beings possess a soul-body duality. Earthly life consists of the divine soul living in a mortal body – described by H. both figuratively as the soul's clothing (cf. also 27, 34, and, perhaps, 39) and literally as flesh (cf. 28).

18 in prima apparatione = *in <mea> prima apparatione* (i.e., in Anima's first appearance on earth, united to a body).

19 ad: "for." **suspiro** < *sub* + *spiro*, *-are*: "to breathe under," i.e., "to sigh."

21 que = *quae*. **edificata es** = CL *aedificata es* (cf. *edificantes* in v. 5). **profunda altitudine:** note the oxymoron.

22 multum amas: cf. *Luke* 7.47 (Jesus' words to the woman who anointed his feet): *propter quod dico tibi remittentur ei peccata multa quoniam dilexit multum cui autem minus dimittitur minus diligit.* ("Therefore I tell you, her sins, which are many, are forgiven, for she loved much; but he who is forgiven little, loves little."). The theme of forgiveness is central to the *Ordo*, and it is characteristic of H.'s technique that she signals it for the first time in a compressed allusion that forces the reader to recall the original context of the phrase.

23 libenter: "willingly," "joyfully"; an important word for H. in this play (cf. also 73, 146 and 222).

23 veniam: (subj.).

24 prebeatis michi = CL *praebeatis mihi*. **osculum:** "kiss"; the phrase *osculum cordis* is metaphorical for "your love"; cf. *Song of Solomon* 1.1: *osculetur me osculo oris sui quia meliora sunt ubera tua vino.* ("O that you would kiss me with the kiss of your mouth, for your breasts are better than wine."). H. digs below the surface of the phrase *osculum oris* ("mouth's kiss") to uncover where the kiss truly originates from. Her creative substitution also eliminates the physical/sexual aspect of love found in her source (by, parodoxically, using the language of physical love) – which is part of her agenda in the play.

25a gravata: "depressed," "troubled." **conqueritur** < *conqueror*, *-i*: "to complain," "lament."

27 vite = CL *vitae*.

28 grave: "grievous." **michi*** = CL *mihi*. **carnem** = *<meam> carnem*.

---

[67] Flanagan (1989, 79) notes that, "[H.] had a very clear notion of the separation of the soul from the body at death and of the fact that they would only be reunited at the Last Judgement. In most sections of the *Liber vitae meritorum* she returns to the idea that final blessedness can only be attained when the soul is reunited with the body after the destruction of the world. Her insistence on the partnership and equal dignity of soul and body (albeit transformed at the resurrection) may . . . be directed against Catharist doctrines." Catharism was a gnostic heresy particularly vigorous in the twelfth century that believed all of creation was inherently evil and only the soul was pure. Interestingly, H.'s play at times can seem to support Catharist ideology.

Virtutes ad Animam illam:
O Anima, voluntate Dei constituta,
et o felix instrumentum, quare tam flebilis es 30
contra hoc quod Deus contrivit in virgenea natura?
Tu debes in nobis superare Diabolum.

Anima illa:
Succurrite michi, adiuvando, ut possim stare!

Scientia Dei ad Animam illam:
Vide quid illud sit quo es induta, filia salvationis,
et esto stabilis, et numquam cades. 35

Infelix, Anima:
O nescio quid faciam,
aut ubi fugiam!
O ve michi, non possum perficere
hoc quod sum induta.
Certe illud volo abicere! 40

Virtutes:
O infelix conscientia,
O misera Anima,
quare abscondis faciem tuam coram creatore tuo?

Scientia Dei:
Tu nescis, nec vides, nec sapis illum qui te constituit.

Anima illa:
Deus creavit mundum: 45
non facio illi iniuriam,
sed volo uti illo!

30 felix instrumentum: Dronke (1994, 182) suggests that H., "may have two senses of instrumentum in mind: seeing Anima as instrumental in achieving her state of bliss, and as the blissful instrument of which God can play his music." **flebilis:** "tearful."

30-1 Aptly paraphrased by Dronke as "Why are you so tearful at the prospect of crushing sin, which God achieved in the maidenly nature of Mary?"

31 hoc = *hoc <malum>*; the "evil" must be sin, or, more specifically for H., the sin of sexual love (cf. *contra carnem pugnare* in v. 28). **contrivit** < *contero*, *-ere*: "to crush," "pulverize."

32 in nobis: Dronke (1994, 182) suggestively notes that, "in terms of the play, Diabolus is in the midst of the Virtues; but the meaning may also be microcosmic: Anima must conquer Diabolus by using the powers (*virtutes*) within herself." **Diabolum:** (EL from the Greek) "the Devil."

33 michi** = CL *mihi*. **adiuvando:** (gerund) "by helping." **stare:** "to stand (firm)."

34 es induta: "you are dressed," "you are wearing"; the reference is to the mortal dress (i.e., her celibate life in her mortal body) that Anima has to complete (*perficere*, 38) before she can win the heavenly *vestem preclaram* (17).

35 esto < *sum*, *esse* (2nd pers. sing. fut. imp. with the same meaning as *es*, the 2nd pers. sing. pres. imp.).

38 ve = CL *vae*.

39 hoc: i.e., "this dress of chastity."

43 abscondis < *abscondo*, *-ere*: "to hide."

43 coram: (+ abl.) "in the presence of"; the image of this verse once again recalls the Garden of Eden (cf. 14 above) where, in *Genesis* 3.8, the story of Adam and Eve's shame brought on by their awareness of their nakedness forces them to hide from God's presence: *et cum audissent vocem Domini Dei deambulantis in paradiso ad auram post meridiem abscondit se Adam et uxor eius a facie Domini Dei in medio ligni paradisi*. ("And when they heard the sound of the Lord God walking in the garden in the cool of the day, Adam and his wife hid themselves from the face of the Lord God among the trees of the garden.")

44 sapis < *sapio*, *-ere*: "to taste," "understand," "have knowledge of." H.'s use of *sapis* here suggests that she is thinking about the Christian sacrament of Communion (the Eucharist) in which one eats bread and drinks wine that, in Christian belief, literally have become the body and blood of Christ. **constituit:** cf. *constituta* in v. 29.

45-7 Anima's philosophical argument can be paraphrased as follows: if God created the material world, including our own physical bodies, then surely he intended us to use and enjoy them. This logical appeal to Nature for the justification of sexual activity is repeated by the Devil in the last words that he speaks in the play (*ubi transis preceptum quod Deus in suavi copula precepi*, 236).

45 illum qui: i.e., Christ.

46 illi: i.e., Deo.

47 uti < *utor*, *uti* (+ abl.): "to use," "enjoy." **illo:** i.e., mundo.

Strepitus Diaboli ad Animam illam:
Fatue, fatue quid prodest tibi laborare?
Respice mundum et amplectetur te magno honore.

Virtutes:
O plangens vox est hec maximi doloris! 50
Ach, ach, quedam mirabilis victoria
in mirabili desiderio Dei surrexit,
in qua delectatio carnis se latenter abscondit,
heu, heu, ubi voluntas crimina nescivit
et ubi desiderium hominis lasciviam fugit. 55
Luge, luge ergo in his, Innocentia,
que in pudore bono integritatem non amisisti,
et que avariciam gutturis antiqui serpentis ibi non devorasti.

47a-9 Anima's defiant decision to abandon the Virtues and enjoy the pleasures of the physical world has provided the psychological opening necessary for the Devil to appear. Shouting (*Strepitus*), the Devil persuades Anima to look to the world (picking up on her use of *mundum*) for honor.

47a Strepitus: (masc. sing. noun) "a confused noise," "din," "clash," "crash," "rattle," "clatter." This word characterizes the type of spoken voice the devil uses as a harsh shout. It may also refer to the fact that the Devil, according to Dronke (1970, 170), "is in chains, and the chains rattle when he moves or speaks."

48 Fatue: "foolishly"; alternatively, *fatue* could be construed as masc. voc. Cf. *Matthew* 5.22 (the only occurrence of *fatue* in the Latin Bible): *ego autem dico vobis quia omnis qui irascitur fratri suo reus erit iudicio qui autem dixerit fratri suo racha reus erit concilio qui autem dixerit fatue reus erit gehennae ignis*. ("But I say to you that everyone who is angry with his brother shall be liable to judgment; whoever insults his brother shall be liable to the council, and whoever says, "You fool!" shall be liable to the fires of Hell."). The thought of *Fatue, fatue quid prodest tibi laborare* may have often been in the minds of nuns such as H. **prodest** < *pro* + *sum, esse*: "to benefit," "use."

49 amplectetur (subj.) < *amplector, -are*: "to embrace." An important word in this play, it includes both the divine embrace (105, 125, 127, 195) and its antithesis, the world's (physical/sexual) embrace (209).

50-5 Dronke (1970, 173) observes that in their song of lamentation the Virtues, "recognize Anima's longing for the divine had contained an element of hubris, and concealed a largely sensual desire for bliss. It is a tragic irony that she who is initially innocent and in her feelings most apt for divine love cannot pass through the next stage of spiritual development without a fault of the will. She is a Psyche who impetuously wants to see the divine Eros before the God is ready to reveal himself."

50 O: a cry of sorrow reflecting the emotional state that the Devil's appearance has precipitated in the Virtues. **hec** = CL *haec*.

51 Ach: "Ah!" (an Old German exclamation). **quedam** = CL *quaedam*.

52 in mirabili desiderio Dei: "in/through her (i.e., the Soul's) wondrous desire for God." **surrexit** = *surrexit <in Anima illa>*.

53 latenter: (adv.) "secretly."

54 crimina < *crimen, -inis* (neut.; often pl. for sing.): "guilt," "crime."

56 luge < *lugo, -ere*: "to mourn," "weep for." **in his:** "for this" (i.e., the thought expressed in v. 53).

57, 58 que* = CL *quae*.

57 integritatem < *integritas, -atis*: "innocence," "purity," "chastity," "perfection."

58 avariciam = CL *avaritiam*. **gutturis** < *guttur, -uris*: "throat," "gullet." **antiqui serpentis:** a common phrase in the play (cf. 143, 172, 206, 227; and also 64, where H. uses the synonymous *dracho* [= CL *draco*]). *Genesis* 3.1 relates the story of the snake who tempts Eve thus: *sed et serpens erat callidior cunctis animantibus terrae quae fecerat Dominus Deus qui dixit ad mulierem cur praecepit vobis Deus ut non comederetis de omni ligno paradisi*. ("Now the serpent was more subtle than all the animals of the earth that the Lord God had made. He said to the woman, "Why did God command you that you should not eat of every tree of paradise?""). **ibi:** "then," "at that time" (i.e., "long ago when Adam and Eve lived in the Garden of Eden).

Diabolus:
Que est hec potestas, quod nullus sit preter Deum? Ego
autem dico, qui voluerit me et voluntatem meam sequi, 60
dabo illi omnia. Tu vero, tuis sequacibus nichil habes
quod dare possis, quia etiam vos omnes nescitis quid sitis.

Humilitas:
Ego cum meis sodalibus bene scio
quod tu es ille antiquus dracho
qui super summum volare voluisti— 65
sed ipse Deus in abyssum proiecit te.

Virtutes:
Nos autem omnes in excelsis habitamus.

59 Que . . . hec*** = CL *Quae . . . haec*. **quod** = *quasi*. **preter** = CL *praeter*.

60 Tu: i.e., Humility. **qui voluerit me et voluntatem meam sequi:** note the alliterative jingle and the double meaning of the phrase, which can be translated as both "whoever should be willing to follow me and my will" and "whoever should want me (i.e., sexually) and be willing to follow my will."

60-1 qui . . . omnia: cf. *Luke* 4.7-8 and *Matthew* 4.9 (the latter is cited here): *et dixit illi haec tibi omnia dabo si cadens adoraveris me*. ("And he [the Devil] said to him [Jesus], "I will give you everything if you should fall down and worship me."")

61 nichil = CL *nihil*.

62 vos omnes nescitis quid sitis: the end of the Devil's speech is rhetorically heightened both by strong alliteration of "s" and by a concluding jingle (*scitis quid sitis*). Dronke (1970, 174) acutely notes in reference to these words that, "in an important sense this is true: they have never asserted themselves, never expressed a personality or will of their own as distinct from God; therefore they have no nature of their own, as Satan has."

63-6 Throughout the play H. characterizes each of her abstract personifications differently (see also the note to 104 below). Humility does not directly answer the Devil's taunting questions (61-2). Instead, since she is far too humble to state who she is and what power she actually bestows upon her followers, she redirects the question by telling the Devil (and the audience) what *he* really is – the ancient serpent who tempted Eve and tried, but failed, to usurp God's power. For the most graphic descriptions in the Bible of Satan's fall, see *Isaiah* 14.12ff. and *Apocalypse* 12.7-12. The idea of Satan's fall is, as Dronke (1994, 182) notes, "a leitmotif throughout Hildegard's writings."

64 dracho = CL *draco* (masc. nom. sing.).

65-6 super summum volare voluisti—sed ipse Deus in abyssum: note the alliteration of these lines. Humility too can play (cf. the phrase *volare voluisti* to v. 60, *voluerit . . . voluntatem*) the Devil's verbal games.

66 ipse Deus abyssum proiecit te: this event is prophesied in *Apocalypse* 20.1-3, though there it is an angel, not God himself, who will hurl the Devil into the bottomless pit. It should be mentioned that this event had not yet happened in H.'s time. From her theologically informed perspective, however, since it had been foretold in the Bible, it will most certainly take place; thus the reason for the perfect tense of *proiecit*. For H., whatever God plans on doing in the future has already been accomplished.

66-7 abyssum . . . excelsis: a neat antithesis that is also effective characterization. H. has the other Virtues, not Humility, make this boast. It should be noted, however, that neither Humility nor the Virtues have yet given an answer to the Devil's attack against them in v. 62.

SCENE 2

Humilitas:
Ego, Humilitas, regina Virtutum, dico:
venite ad me, Virtutes, et enutriam vos
ad requirendam perditam dragmam 70
et ad coronandum in perseverantia felicem.

Virtutes:
O gloriosa regina, et o suavissima mediatrix,
libenter venimus.

Humilitas:
Ideo, dilectissime filie,
teneo vos in regali talamo. 75

SCENE 2 (68-158)

In this lengthy scene each of the sixteen Virtues steps forward and briefly characterizes herself. The structure of this dramatically static but thematically important section centers around five Virtues –Humility, Charity, Obedience, Faith, and World-Rejection – who invite the others (*venio* and its compound *pervenire* are very common) to join with them in a spiritual sisterhood. This sense of community among the various Virtues, which continues to grow throughout this section, is broken only once by a brief and sardonic interjection of the Devil early on (84-5). After this interruption the scene reaches a climax in a series of extended and elaborate metaphors describing the nun's spiritual union with Christ. Blending sensual images of physical love from the *Song of Solomon* (75, 90, 104, 125, 129, 131, and 154) with images of flowers, growth, light, and water (cf. 77, 95, 106-111, 135, and 156), H. reveals the joyous beauty behind her vision of the nun's "marriage" to Christ. And yet a discordant note is repeatedly struck in this calm sea of spiritual ecstasy with the recurrent image of battle (119-21, 132, 143, 146-7, 155) against the corrupting forces of the Devil (112, 133).

68 regina: that Humility is "queen of the virtues" is another of H.'s oxymorons.

69 enutriam < *enutrio, -are*: "to nourish," "raise."

70 ad requirendam: (*ad* + gerundive = purpose clause). **dragmam** = CL *drachmam* (a Greek silver coin); cf. *Luke* 15.8-10: *aut quae mulier habens dragmas decem si perdiderit dragmam unam nonne accendit lucernam et everrit domum et quaerit diligenter donec inveniat* 9 *et cum invenerit convocat amicas et vicinas dicens congratulamini mihi quia inveni dragmam quam perdideram* 10 *ita dico vobis gaudium erit coram angelis Dei super uno peccatore paenitentiam agente*. ("Or what woman, having ten silver coins, if she loses one coin, does not light a lamp and sweep the house and seek diligently until she finds it? 9 And when she has found it, she calls together her friends and neighbors, saying, "Rejoice with me for I have found the coin which I had lost." Just so, I tell you, there will be more joy in heaven over one sinner who repents than over ninety-nine righteous persons who need no repentance."). This parable represents one of the few times in the Bible that God is (metaphorically) described as female.

71 ad coronandum . . . felicem = *ad coronandum eam quae est felix in perseverantia*.

72 mediatrix: H. creates a fem. noun from the CL masc. *mediator* since all of her Virtues are feminine.

74 dilectissime filie* = CL *dilectissimae filiae*.

75 talamo = CL *thalamo*: "wedding-chamber," "bedroom"; the expression *in regali talamo* means "marriage with Christ," which was the traditional view of a nun's life.

Karitas:
Ego Karitas, flos amabilis—
venite ad me, Virtutes, et perducam vos
in candidam lucem floris virge.

Virtutes:
O dilectissime flos, ardenti desiderio currimus ad te.

Timor Dei:
Ego, Timor Dei, vos felicissimas filias preparo 80
ut inspiciatis in Deum vivum et non pereatis.

Virtutes:
O Timor, valde utilis es nobis:
habemus enim perfectum studium numquam a te separari.

Diabolus:
Euge! Euge! Quis est tantus timor? Et quis est tantus amor?
Ubi est pugnator, et ubi est remunerator? Vos nescitis quid colitis. 85

Virtutes:
Tu autem exterritus es per summum iudicem,
quia, inflatus superbia, mersus es in gehennam.

76 Ego Karitas = *Ego <sum> Karitas*. **Karitas**: a prominent figure in H.'s theology who embodies several different allegorical characters: the Bride of the *Song of Solomon*; Divine Wisdom; and Divine Love. She is also a central character in a vision from H.'s *Liber Vitae Meritorum* ("Book of Life's Merits"), where she says: "I am the air; I nourish all green and growing life . . . I am skilled in every breath of the Spirit . . . so, I pour out limpid streams." Newman (1987, 79) believes that in H.'s theological view, "[Karitas] is God's love for the world as well as the world's for God. She is the love that beckons us to wonder but also the love that summons us to work." **flos:** a recurring image in this scene (see also 78, 79, 107-111, 135).

78 virge = CL *virgae*: "rod"; for *floris virge*, cf. *Isaiah* 11.1: *et egredietur virga de radice Iesse et flos de radice eius ascendet*. ("There shall come forth a rod from the root of Jesse, and a flower shall grow out of his roots."). Dronke (1994, 150) notes that, "Karitas promises to lead the other Virtues *in candidam lucem floris virge* – "into the radiant light of the flower of the rod" (78). Aaron's rod (*virga*) that bursts into flower (cf. *Numbers* 17) is the traditional figura of Mary (*virgo*) bringing forth the flower that is Christ – thus the complex metaphor, with its double genitive, is a promise to lead the Virtues into the luminous realm of the incarnation." **candidam:** one of H.'s favorite adjectives (see also 114, 135, and 180).

82 valde: (adv.) "greatly."

83 studium < *studium, -i*: "desire," "longing."

84-5 The Devil continues his alliterative-jingle ways.

84 Euge: (EL from the Greek) "Bravo"; Dronke (1994, 183) notes that, "the double *euge* is used as a derisive shout in *Ezekiel* 25.3. Diabolus here mocks both fear of God and love of God. With *Ubi est pugnator* . . . he is saying, there is no struggle, and no one to reward the winner in a struggle."

85 remunerator: (ML) "prize-giver," "rewarder." **Vos nescitis quid colitis:** cf. v. 62 above. **colitis** < *colo, -ere*: "to worship."

86 To counter his boast that he knows no *timor*, the Virtues remind the Devil that he was afraid when God (*summum iudicem*) threw him into the abyss.

87-8 superbia . . . Obedientia: another of H.'s antitheses.

87 superbia: (abl.); in Letter 58 of H.'s correspondence, *Superbia* is equated with Satan: "*Superbia* swore against me [i.e., Karitas] and wanted to fly higher than the stars, but I threw him into the abyss." In the eyes of H. and other Christians, the Devil, lacking any humility (*inflatus superbia*), set up his own fall.

87 Gehennam: "Hell"; the Aramaic word *Gehenna* only occurs in the Bible in the New Testament (its first appearance is *Mark* 9.43-8). According to Jesus in the synoptic gospels, it is the place where sinners are punished after death.

Obedientia:
Ego lucida Obedientia—
venite ad me, pulcherrime filie, et reducam vos
ad patriam et ad osculum regis. 90

Virtutes:
O dulcissima vocatrix,
nos decet in magno studio pervenire ad te.

Fides:
Ego Fides, speculum vite:
venerabiles filie, venite ad me
et ostendo vobis fontem salientem. 95

Virtutes:
O serena, speculata, habemus fiduciam
pervenire ad verum fontem per te.

Spes:
Ego sum dulcis conspectrix viventis oculi,
quam fallax torpor non decipit—
unde vos, o tenebre, non potestis me obnubilare. 100

Virtutes:
O vivens vita, et o suavis consolatrix,
tu mortifera mortis vincis
et vidente oculo clausuram celi aperis.

88 lucida (adj.) *lucidus, -a, -um*: "shining."

89 pulcherrime filie** = CL *pulcherrimae filiae.*

90 osculum regis: H.'s second allusion to *Song of Solomon* 1.1 (cf. v. 24 above and note *ad loc.*). This time, however, by changing one word (*regis* for *cordis*), H. has extended the allusion to include vv. 2-3 as well: 1 *osculetur me osculo oris sui quia meliora sunt ubera tua vino* 2 *fragrantia unguentis optimis oleum effusum nomen tuum ideo adulescentulae dilexerunt te* 3 *trahe me post te curremus introduxit me rex in cellaria sua exultabimus et laetabimur in te memores uberum tuorum super vinum recti diligunt te.* ("O that you would kiss me with the kiss of your mouth, for your breasts are better than wine, 2 your anointing oils are fragrant, your name is oil poured out; therefore the maidens love you. 3 Draw me after you, let us make haste. The king has brought me into his chambers. We will exult and rejoice in you; we will extol your love more than wine; rightly do they love you.")

93 speculum vite* = CL *speculum vitae*; this phrase first appears in the early Roman comic playwrights Plautus (*Epidicus* 383-4) and Terence (*Adelphoe* 415). The latter was especially popular in the Middle Ages, and may have (indirectly) been H.'s source.

95 salientem < *salio, salire*: "to leap," "spring"; cf. *John* 4.14: *sed aqua quam dabo ei fiet in eo fons aquae salientis in vitam aeternam.* ("But the water that I [Jesus] will give to him will become in him a spring of water welling up to eternal life.")

96 speculata: (ML) "watcher"; "mirror-like."

98 viventis oculi: cf. v. 7 above; Dronke (1994, 183) believes that, "[H.] probably intends the genitive to have both subjective and objective force: Spes gazes upon God's eye, and she is the gazing of God's eye, "the life of life" (cf. 101, 103)."

99-100 H. uses the synonymous word-pairings of *fallax . . . decipit* and *tenebre . . . obnubilare* for emphasis.

100 tenebre = CL *tenebrae*. **obnubilare:** (ML) "to cloud."

102 mortifera: (neut. pl. adj.; compound of *mors + fero*) "lethal/deadly <shafts>."

103 oculo: this refers either to the "eye of Hope" or it is a metaphor for "God" (see vv. 7 and 98 and notes *ad loc.*). **clausuram:** "gate," "lock." **celi** = CL *caeli.*

Castitas:
O Virginitas, in regali talamo stas.
O quam dulciter ardes in amplexibus regis, 105
cum te sol perfulget
ita quod nobilis flos tuus numquam cadet.
O virgo nobilis, te numquam inveniet umbra in cadente flore!

Virtutes:
Flos campi cadit vento, pluvia spargit eum.
O Virginitas, tu permanes in symphoniis supernorum civium: 110
unde es suavis flos qui numquam aresces.

Innocentia:
Fugite, oves, spurcicias Diaboli!

Virtutes:
Has te succurrente fugiemus.

Contemptus Mundi:
Ego, Contemptus Mundi, sum candor vite.
O misera terre peregrinatio 115
in multis laboribus—te dimitto.
O Virtutes, venite ad me
et ascendamus ad fontem vite!

Virtutes:
O gloriosa domina, tu semper habes certamina Christi,
o magna virtus, que mundum conculcas, 120
unde etiam victoriose in celo habitas.

104-9 The language and imagery employed in these lines are sexually charged, but metaphorically transferred (if only slightly) from the physical plane to the spiritual. The union of a virgin nun to her bridegroom Christ both is and is not, in H.'s view, like that of a husband and wife.

104 (and 112) Dronke (1994, 183) observes that, "Neither Castitas nor Innocentia declare themselves, like the other virtues. Hildegard presents them as timid figures, so that Castitas celebrates Maidenhood rather than herself, and Innocentia utters only the briefest words of encouragement, to the *oves* – presumably the audience, or *omnes homines* (267). The expression *oves* foreshadows the allusions to the parable of the lost sheep (*Luke* 15.3-7) at the opening of the next scene (160)."

104 O Virginitas, in regali talamo stas: cf. v. 75 above and note *ad loc*. Concerning this verse, Newman (1987, 222-3) mentions the interesting story that, "In 1151, soon after Hildegard had completed the Scivias, her beloved secretary Richardis von Stade was elected abbess of Birsim (now Bassum) through the influence of her brother, Archbishop Hartwig of Bremen. Hildegard contested this election by all possible means to prevent her favorite nun's departure. Nonetheless, Richardis accepted the office and left the Rupertsberg for Birsim, where she fell ill and died less than a year later. After her death, Hildegard wrote Hartwig to console him for their mutual loss . . . add[ing] that, while Richardis was still alive, she had seen her in a vision and heard a voice saying, "O Virginity, you stand in the royal bridal chamber!"" It seems likely that H. composed this speech of Chastity and its choral response (109-11) in memory of her departed friend who, Newman (1987, 223) believes, "was meant to play the role of this Virtue in the original performance.

107 Nobilis flos tuus numquam cadet: *flos tuus cadet* is metaphorical for the loss of a woman's virginity (cf. the English "deflower").

108 te numquam . . . flore: the image is abbreviated and difficult to understand; perhaps, "never will the shadow <cast> by the falling flower come upon you." The "shadow" (*umbra*) here is apparently a metaphor for the loss of one's virginity.

109 Flos campi: cf. *Song of Solomon* 2.1: *ego flos campi et lilium convallium*. ("I am a flower of the field and a lily of the valleys.") **spargit** < *spargo, -ere*: "to splash" "sprinkle." **pluvia** < *pluvia, -ae*: "rain," "shower" (metaphorical for semen?).

110 symphoniis: an important word for H. (cf. also v. 194 and see **1 Hildegard of Bingen (1098-1179)**, above). **supernorum** < (adj.) *supernus, -a, -um*: "celestial," "heavenly."

111 aresces < *aresco, -ere*: "to grow dry," "wither."

112 oves: cf. *Luke* 15.3-7 (and see note to v. 13 above) for the parable of the lost sheep. **spurcicias** = CL *spurcitias* < *spurcitia, -ae*: "filth," "excrement," "smut."

113 te succurrente: (abl. abs. with conditional force; i.e., "if . . .").

113a Contemptus Mundi: "World-Rejection," "Contempt for the World."

114 vite** = CL *vitae*.

115 terre = CL *terrae*.

118 fontem: cf. vv. 95 and 97 above.

119 habes: i.e., "you fight."

120 conculcas < *conculco, -are*: "to trample under foot," "despise"; cf. also vv. 132, 143, and 229 below.

121, 122 celo* = CL *caelo*.

Amor Celestis:
Ego aurea porta in celo fixa sum:
qui per me transit
numquam amaram petulantiam in mente sua gustabit.

Virtutes:
O filia regis, tu semper es in amplexibus quos mundus fugit. 125
O quam suavis est tua dilectio in summo Deo!

Disciplina:
Ego sum amatrix simplicium morum qui turpia opera nesciunt;
sed semper in regum regem aspicio
et amplector eum in honore altissimo.

Virtutes:
O tu angelica socia, tu es valde ornata 130
in regalibus nuptiis.

Verecundia:
Ego obtenebro et fugo atque conculco
omnes spurcicias Diaboli.

Virtutes:
Tu es in edificatione celestis Ierusalem,
florens in candidis liliis. 135

Misericordia:
O quam amara est illa duricia que non cedit in mentibus,
misericorditer dolori succurrens!
Ego autem omnibus dolentibus manum porrigere volo.

Virtutes:
O laudabilis mater peregrinorum,
tu semper erigis illos, 140
atque ungis pauperes et debiles.

Victoria:
Ego Victoria velox et fortis pugnatrix sum—
in lapide pugno, serpentem antiquum conculco.

122 Celestis** = CL *Caelestis.*

124 numquam . . . gustabit: note the strong alliteration (especially of "m" and "am") and the mixture of the physical and the mental. **petulantiam** < *petulantia, -ae*: "rebelliousness," "petulance."

126 dilectio: (EL) "(Christian) love." **dilectio in summo Deo:** Dronke (1994, 183) believes that, "the ambiguity may well be deliberate: Amor Celestis exists in the highest God and proceeds from him – or again, is a quality that opens heaven to mortals and comes to rest in God."

127 nesciunt: Discipline repeats the Devil's use of *nescio* at vv. 62 and 85 – but with a twist.

131 in regalibus nuptiis: cf. vv. 75 (and note *ad loc.*) and 104 (*in regali talamo*). Here the "bedroom" (*talamus*) becomes the more explicit "wedding" (*nuptiae*).

132 obtenebro . . . fugo . . . conculco: *Verecundia* ("Shamefastness") aggresively takes the offensive. **obtenebro** < *obtenebro, -are*: "to cover over"; cf. v. 100 (*o tenebre... obnubilare*), where the reference was to Hope's claim that the Devil's darkness was unable to envelop her in a black cloud; here the image is reversed, for Shamefastness claims she will be able to "cover over" the Devil. **fugo** < *fugo, -are*: "to cause to flee," "drive off," "put to flight."

132-3 conculco omnes spurcicias Diaboli: cf. *Genesis* 3.15: *inimicitias ponam inter te et mulierem et semen tuum et semen illius ipsa conteret caput tuum et tu insidiaberis calcaneo eius.* ("I [God] will put enmity between you [i.e., the Serpent] and the woman, and between your offspring and hers; she will strike your head, and you will ambush her heel."). Christians understood the "she" (*ipsa*) to be the Virgin Mary, and often depicted her in art crushing a serpent beneath her heel.

134 Ierusalem: (indecl. noun; here = gen. sing.). **edificatione**** = CL *aedificatione* < *aedificatio, -onis* (cf. vv. 5 and 21). **celestis Ierusalem:** (the phrase is gen. sing.); cf. *Hebrews* 12.22 (*Hierusalem caelestem*), the only occurrence of this phrase in the New Testament. The idea of "Heavenly Jerusalem" is ultimately derived from *Isaiah* 65.18.

136 duricia = CL *duritia* < *duritia, -ae*: "harshness." **cedit** < *cedo, -ere*: "to go away," "leave."

137 misericorditer: note the pun on the speaker's name (called in English a "Tom Swifty").

138 porrigere < *porrigo, -ere*: "to reach out"; cf. v. 269, the final line of the play.

139 peregrinorum < *peregrinus, -i*: "foreigner," "stranger," "exile."

140 erigis: < *erigo, -ere*: "to raise up."

141 ungis: < *ungo, -ere*: "to anoint." **pauperes et debiles:** Dronke (1994, 183) notes that, "Misericordia's annointing of the poor and weak recalls the action of the Good Samaritan, *misericordia motus* (*Luke* 10.33-4)."

142 pugnatrix: in a delayed reply to the Devil's question in vv. 84-5, *Ubi est pugnator?*, Victory steps forward and declares, "I am the *pugnatrix*." The shift to the feminine noun is significant, since it negates the Devil's belief that only a male champion could fight for the (female) Virtues.

143 in lapide: "with a stone"; the phrase recalls the battle between David and Goliath (1 *Samuel* 17.49). **serpentem antiquum conculco:** cf. vv. 58 and 132-3 (and note *ad loc.*). In one of H.'s more compressed analogies, Victory is presented as both David and Mary in the same verse.

Virtutes:
O dulcissima bellatrix, in torrente fonte
qui absorbuit lupum rapacem— 145
o gloriosa coronata, nos libenter
militamus tecum contra illusorem hunc.

Discretio:
Ego Discretio sum lux et dispensatrix omnium creaturarum,
indifferentia Dei, quam Adam a se fugavit per lasciviam morum.

Virtutes:
O pulcherrima mater, quam dulcis et quam suavis es, 150
quia nemo confunditur in te.

Pacientia:
Ego sum columpna que molliri non potest,
quia fundamentum meum in Deo est.

Virtutes:
O firma que stas in caverna petre,
et o gloriosa bellatrix que suffers omnia! 155

Humilitas:
O filie Israhel, sub arbore suscitavit vos Deus,
unde in hoc tempore recordamini plantationis sue.
Gaudete ergo, filie Syon!

144-5 The Virtues address Victory and seem to describe the battle in which she defeats Satan (the "greedy wolf") "in the scorching fountain," the antithesis of the "leaping fountain" of v. 95.

144 dulcissima bellatrix: another (apparent) oxymoron. **torrente** (adj.) < *torrens, -entis*: "scorching."

145 absorbuit: < *absorbeo, -ere*: "to swallow up," "devour." **lupum** < *lupus, -i*: "wolf."

147 militamus: cf. v. 25.

148 dispensatrix: (ML fem. for CL masc. *dispensator*) "moderator," "provider," "treasurer."

149 indifferentia (adj. as noun.) < *indifferens, -entis*: "impartiality." **per lasciviam:** "by acting rebelliously/irresponsibly." The primary meaning of *lascivia*, however, is "lewdness," "sexual impropriety"; thus the phrase can also be translated "by acting wantonly." According to H., Adam drove Indiscretion away when he listened to his wife and ate fruit from the tree of knowledge of good and evil from which God had commanded him not to eat (*Genesis* 3.6, 17). Unlike H., however, the majority of Christian theologians would have claimed that it was Eve who primarily had driven Indiscretion away when, after listening to the serpent's suggestion to disobey God's one command, she first ate of the fruit of the tree before sharing some of it with her husband (*Genesis* 3.1-6).

150-54 An extensive reworking of *Song of Solomon* 2.14: *columba mea in foraminibus petrae in caverna maceriae ostende mihi faciem tuam sonet vox tua in auribus meis vox enim tua dulcis et facies tua decora*. ("O my dove, in the clefts of the rock, in the cave of the cliff, reveal to me your face, let your voice sound in my ears, for your voice is swift and your face beautiful.") H. has transformed the "dove" (i.e., the bride) who hides in the rocky cavern into a "glorious warrior."

151 confunditur < *confundo, -ere*: "to confound," "confuse," "defy."

151a Pacientia = CL *Patientia*.

152 columpna = CL *columna*. **molliri** < *mollio, -ire*: "to make soft." The pairing of *columpna* and *molliri* borders on the surreal.

154 petre = CL *petrae* < *petra, -ae*: "rock."

155 suffers < *suffero, -ere*: "to endure."

156 The image of being raised up from beneath a tree is a metaphor for Christ's redemptive suffering on the cross. **Israhel:** (indecl. noun; here = gen. sing.). **sub arbore suscitavit:** cf. *Song of Solomon* 8.5: *quae est ista quae ascendit de deserto deliciis affluens et nixa super dilectum suum sub arbore malo suscitavi te ibi corrupta est mater tua ibi violata est genetrix tua*. ("Who is that coming up from the wilderness, flowing with delights, leaning upon her beloved? Under the apple tree I raised you up. There your mother was corrupted, there she who bore you was violated [or "lost her virginity"].")

157 recordamini: (+ gen.). **plantationis sue** = CL *plantationis suae*: "its planting", i.e., "the time when God planted it." **Syon:** (indecl. noun; here = gen. sing.); an alternative name for Jerusalem; *Psalm* 87.3 calls Zion (the more common spelling in Latin and English) the "city of God." 2 *Esdras* 13.36 speaks of it in referring to the heavenly Jerusalem that would ultimately replace the earthly one (cf. also *Apocalypse* 21.1-17). In *Hebrews* 12.22, Zion refers to the "new covenant" of Jesus.

SCENE 3

Virtutes:
Heu, heu, nos Virtutes plangamus et lugeamus,
quia ovis domini fugit vitam! 160

Querela Anime penitentis et Virtutes invocantis:
O vos regales Virtutes, quam speciose
et quam fulgentes estis in summo sole,
et quam dulcis est vestra mansio—
et ideo, o ve michi, quia a vobis fugi!

Virtutes:
O fugitive, veni, veni ad nos, et Deus suscipiet te. 165

Anima illa:
Ach! Ach! Fervens dulcedo absorbuit me in peccatis,
et ideo non ausa sum intrare.

Virtutes:
Noli timere nec fugere,
quia pastor bonus querit in te perditam ovem suam.

Anima illa:
Nunc est michi necesse ut suscipiatis me, 170
quoniam in vulneribus feteo
quibus antiquus serpens me contaminavit.

Virtutes:
Curre ad nos, et sequere vestigia illa
in quibus numquam cades in societate nostra,
et Deus curabit te. 175

SCENE 3 (159-208)

Scene 2 ended with Humility's call to joy. The beginning of Scene 3 disrupts this hopeful mood with the initial lament of the Virtues for Anima (159-60), who now returns, penitent and filled with grief, from her visit to the world (161-4). The Virtues and Humility immediately comfort her in an emotional reunion where forgiveness is asked and given (165-89). In a metaphorical exploration of the Christian idea of moral redemption, H. combines the traditional equation of sickness equaling sin (171-2, 177, 187) with the image of the wounded Christ, the great doctor who (paradoxically) suffered sacrificial wounds so that one's own might be healed (190, 196-7). The scene concludes with the exultant thanksgiving hymn "O Vivens Fons" (198-208), a song that extends the power of God's forgiveness from one sinner, Anima, to all sinners.

160 ovis domini fugit vitam: cf. *Luke* 15.3-7 (and vv. 13 and 104 with notes *ad loc*.).

160-165 fugit . . . fugi . . . fugitive: note the repetition.

160a Anime = CL *Animae*. **penitentis** = CL *paenitentis*.

161 speciose (adj.) = CL *speciosae* < *speciosus*, *-a*, *-um*: "beautiful," "graceful."

162 fulgentes estis in summo sole: cf. v. 4.

164 ve* michi = CL *vae mihi*.

165 fugitive: H. treats *fugitivus* as both masc. and fem.

166 dulcedo: (nom. sing.) "sweetness"; the phrase *fervens dulcedo* is an euphemism for sex. **absorbuit:** cf. v. 145.

167 ausa sum < *audeo*, *-ere*: "to dare."

168 Noli: (pres. imp. of *nolo*, *nolle*); the imperative here simply negates the two infinitives *timere* and *fugere*. Dronke (1994, 183) notes that, "the expression *noli timere* is characteristically used by angels in *Luke*: to Zachary (1.13), to Mary (1.30), and to the shepherds (2.10)."

169 querit = CL *quaerit*; for Jesus as the "good shepherd," cf. *Luke* 15.3-7 (see notes to vv. 13, 104, and 160) and especially *John* 10.11: *ego sum pastor bonus bonus pastor animam suam dat pro ovibus* ("I am the good shepherd, the good shepherd gives his own life for his sheep") and 10.14: *ego sum pastor bonus et cognosco meas et cognoscunt me meae* ("I am the good shepherd, and I know my own and my own know me.").

170 michi** = CL *mihi*. **Nunc est michi necesse:** "There is now necessity to me," i.e., "Now I need your help."

171 feteo < CL *foeteo*, *-ere*: "to stink."

173-5 These verses metaphorically restate the central Christian message that all can be forgiven, no matter what one has done, as long as one asks for forgiveness.

173 vestigia < *vestigium*, *-i*: "step."

Penitens Anima ad Virtutes: 175a
Ego peccator qui fugi vitam:
plenus ulceribus veniam ad vos,
ut prebeatis michi scutum redemptionis.

O tu omnis milicia regine,
et o vos, candida lilia ipsius, cum rosea purpura, 180
inclinate vos ad me, quia peregrina a vobis exulavi,
et adiuvate me, ut in sanguine filii Dei possim surgere.

Virtutes:
O Anima fugitiva, esto robusta,
et indue te arma lucis.

Anima illa:
Et o vera medicina, Humilitas, prebe michi auxilium, 185
quia superbia in multis viciis fregit me,
multas cicatrices michi imponens.
Nunc fugio ad te, et ideo suscipe me.

Humilitas:
O omnes Virtutes, suscipite lugentem peccatorem,
in suis cicatricibus, propter vulnera Christi, 190
et perducite eum ad me.

Virtutes:
Volumus te reducere et nolumus te deserere,
Et omnis celestis milicia gaudet super te—
Ergo decet nos in symphonia sonare.

Humilitas:
O misera filia, volo te amplecti, 195
quia magnus medicus dura et amara vulnera
propter te passus est.

175a Penitens* = CL *Paenitens*.

178 prebeatis* michi = CL *praebeatis mihi*; cf. v. 24. **scutum** < *scutum*, *-i*: "shield"; the image is from *Ephesians* 6.16 (*scutum fidei*). H., however, modifies the Pauline phrase for her own purposes (contrast v. 184, where she keeps the original Pauline phrase since its imagery fits that which she has created for this play).

179 milicia = CL *militia*. **regine** = CL *reginae*.

180 candida lilia: cf. v. 135, *in candidis liliis*. **cum rosea purpura:** "with rosy-colored purple," i.e., "with crimson roses."

181 peregrina a vobis exulavi = *ex(s)ulavi me a vobis <velut> peregrina*; note how H. creates emphasis by using synonymous terms (*peregrina*, *exulavi*).

183 esto: cf. v. 35.

184 arma lucis: cf. *Romans* 13.12: *nox praecessit dies autem adpropiavit abiciamus ergo opera tenebrarum et induamur arma lucis*. ("The night is far gone, the day is now at hand. Let us then cast off the works of darkness and put on the armor of light.")

185 prebe** = CL *praebe* (cf. vv. 24 and 178).

186 superbia: cf. v. 87. **viciis** = CL *vitiis*. **fregit** < *frango*, *-ere*: "to break."

187 cicatrices < *cicatrix*, *-icis*: "scar," "wound"; cf. *Psalm* 37.6: *conputruerunt et tabuerunt cicatrices meae a facie insipientiae meae*. ("My wounds grow foul and fester, because of my foolishness.")

189 peccatorem (EL) < *peccator*, *-oris*: "sinner."

191 eum = *eam*; the masc. pronoun is used because of attraction to *peccatorem*, which H. treats as being of common gender.

192 Note the alliteration and internal rhyme used for emphasis.

193 Cf. *Luke* 15.7: *dico vobis quod ita gaudium erit in caelo super uno peccatore paenitentiam habente quam super nonaginta novem iustis qui non indigent paenitentia* ("So I tell you that there will be <more> joy in heaven over one sinner who repents than over ninety-nine righteous people who need no repentance.") and 15.10: *ita dico vobis gaudium erit coram angelis Dei super uno peccatore paenitentiam agente* ("So I tell you there will be joy before the angels of God over one sinner who repents."). **milicia*** = CL *militia*.

Virtutes:
O vivens fons, quam magna est suavitas tua,
qui faciem istorum in te non amisisti,
sed acute previdisti 200
quomodo eos de angelico casu abstraheres
qui se estimabant illud habere
quod non licet sic stare;
unde gaude, filia Syon,
quia Deus tibi multos reddit 205
quos serpens de te abscidere voluit,
qui nunc in maiori luce fulgent
quam prius illorum causa fuisset.

SCENE 4

Diabolus:
Que es, aut unde venis? Tu amplexata es me, et ego
foras eduxi te. Sed nunc in reversione tua confundis me— 210
ego autem pugna mea deiciam te!

Penitens Anima:
Ego omnes vias meas malas esse cognovi, et ideo fugi a te.
Modo autem, o illusor, pugno contra te.
Inde tu, o regina Humilitas, tuo medicamine adiuva me!

Humilitas ad Victoriam:
O Victoria, que istum in celo superasti, 215
curre cum militibus tuis
et omnes ligate Diabolum hunc!

Victoria ad Virtutes:
O fortissimi et gloriosissimi milites, venite,
et adiuvate me istum fallacem vincere.

Virtutes:
O dulcissima bellatrix, in torrente fonte 220
qui absorbuit lupum rapacem—
o gloriosa coronata, nos libenter
militamus tecum contra illusorem hunc.

198 vivens fons: cf. v. 95.

199 faciem (fem. noun; only the nom. *facies*, acc. *faciem* and abl. *facie* forms are used for the sing.): "face," "look," "gaze." **amisisti** < *amitto*, *-ere*: "to send away," "dismiss"; "to lose," "let slip"; "to reject."

200 previdisti = CL *praevidisti*.

201 de angelico casu: "from the angelic fall" refers to the banishment of Satan and his followers from heaven (cf. *Apocalypse* 12.7-10) and is a compressed way of saying "from suffering the same fate as those angels who fell from heaven." **abstraheres** < *abstraho*, *-ere*: "to pull away," "drag away," "remove."

202 estimabant = CL *aestimabant* < *aestimo*, *-are*: "to estimate," "believe." **illud:** "that (power)."

203 stare < *sto*, *-are*: "to stand," "stand firm," "continue," "exist" (cf. v. 33).

204 unde: "for this reason." **filia Syon:** for *Syon*, cf. v. 158; here, however, the phrase means "daughter Jerusalem," and refers solely to the new, heavenly Jerusalem (cf. *Apocalypse* 21.10ff.). **multos:** "many people," i.e., "many souls."

206 abscidere = CL *abscindere*: "to tear off," "break off," "divide."

208 causa < *causa*, *-ae*: "condition," "state."

SCENE 4 (209-51)

The Devil interrupts the entourage of Virtues leading back the repentant Anima and threatens the latter with violence (209-11). Anima, now energized by her community of Virtues, responds in kind, daring to fight the Devil on his own terms (cf. *pugna*, 210 and *pugno*, 213). She then calls on Humility for aid who, in turn, enjoins Victory along with the rest of the Virtues to enter the combat against the Devil (214-24). They attack and quickly succeed in chaining him (225-8). At this point H.'s play dramatically and theologically takes an unexpected twist as Chastity steps forth and boasts that she too, like Victory earlier (143), had trod on the serpent's head via Christs' miraculous birth from the virgin Mary (229) – thus fulfilling God's prophecy in *Genesis* 3.15 (cf. vv. 132-3 and note *ad loc.*) The Devil, however, rejoins with a powerful critique of virginity that draws on both nature (pleasure) and the divine will (God's command for Adam and Eve to procreate, *Genesis* 1.28). At first Chastity appears to be taken off guard by the Devil's attack on the material and theological bases for her status as a Christian virtue (238-9). She quickly recovers, however, and articulates her own clearly thought out theology of salvation: the incarnation was not a human birth but the beginning of the reintegration in God of the human race (240-1). The scene ends with a chorus in which the Virtues give praise and thanks for the "great counsel" of God that devised the plan of salvation through which they may steer God's children (i.e., human souls) "into the heavenly Jerusalem" (242-51).

209 Que es: the Devil's question to Anima repeats that which he earlier spoke to the Virtues in vv. 61-2 and 85.

210 confundis: cf. v. 151. **deiciam** < *deicio*, *-ere*: "to throw down."

209-11 In a rather desperate move the Devil abandons verbal sophistry in his bid to win Anima back and decides to resort to violence. But, as he will shortly find out (vv. 215ff.), two can play at that game.

211a Penitens** = CL *Paenitens*.

220-3 = 144-7 (The Virtues repeat their acclamation of *Victoria*).

Humilitas:
Ligate ergo istum, o Virtutes preclare!

Virtutes:
O regina nostra, tibi parebimus, 225
et precepta tua in omnibus adimplebimus.

Victoria:
Gaudete, o socii, quia antiquus serpens ligatus est!

Virtutes:
Laus tibi, Christe, rex angelorum!

Castitas:
In mente altissimi, o Satana, caput tuum conculcavi,
et in virginea forma dulce miraculum colui, 230
ubi filius Dei venit in mundum:
unde deiectus es in omnibus spoliis tuis,
et nunc gaudeant omnes qui habitant in celis,
quia venter tuus confusus est.

Diabolus:
Tu nescis quid colis, quia venter tuus vacuus est pulcra 235
forma de viro sumpta—ubi transis preceptum quod Deus
in suavi copula precepit; unde nescis quid sis!

224 preclare = CL *praeclarae*.

226 precepta = CL *praecepta*. **in omnibus:** "in all ways," i.e., "utterly," "totally," "completely." **adimplebimus** < *ad* + *impleo*, *-ere* (a LL compound).

227 Cf. *Apocalypse* 20.2: *et adprehendit draconem serpentem antiquum qui est diabolus et Satanas et ligavit eum per annos mille*. ("And he seized the dragon, the ancient serpent, who is the Devil and Satan, and bound him for a thousand years.")

229-34 Chastity assumes the role of Mary, the mother of Jesus, and declares how she alone, as a virgin, saved the world by bringing into it the savior, her son Jesus Christ.

229 In mente altissimi: *in mente altissimi (Dei)* must mean something like "in accordance with God's prediction/plan" (cf. vv. 132-3 and note *ad loc*. for this prediction). **Satana:** the only time the Devil is so named in the play. *Satanas* (an indeclinable masc. noun in Latin, with the exception of the vocative) is an Aramaic word that means "the adversary." **caput tuum conculcavi:** cf. vv. 132-3 and 143.

234 venter: "stomach," "belly"; the word metaphorically refers generally to the Devil's insatiable appetite for evil (cf. also v. 58: *avariciam gutturis antiqui serpentis ibi non devorasti*), and specifically to sexual nature in all its corruption.

235-7 The Devil's final words in the play are philosophically and theologically provocative. He declares to the Virtues that sex (and, consequently, motherhood) is a wonderful, human experience enjoined by God. In essence, the Devil is quoting scripture (cf. *Genesis* 1.28: *benedixitque illis Deus et ait crescite et multiplicamini et replete terram* ["And God blessed them and told them, "Be fruitful and multiply, and fill the earth.""]). Note too his clever recycling of the word *venter* that was just used against him in v. 234. The very last words which he speaks – *unde nescis quid sis* – restate what he said to Anima and the Virtues in Scene 1 (*quia etiam vos omnes nescitis quid sitis*, 62). The Devil thus claims that their lifestyle choice (virginity) is unnatural and irreligious. His ideas can, in a sense, be seen as representative of medieval society's views concerning the "natural" role and function of women.

235 vacuus: (+ abl.).

235-6 pulcra forma . . . sumpta: (abls.). **sumpta** < *sumo*, *-are*: "to take," "receive." **preceptum* . . . precepit**** = CL *praeceptum . . . praecepit*; note how the cognates create an alliterative jingle which reinforces the Devil's message (sarcastic thought its tone may be) that they are disobeying the first command God gave to humans.

236 ubi: "in this."

Castitas:
Quomodo posset me hoc tangere
quod tua suggestio polluit per immundiciam incestus?
Unum virum protuli, qui genus humanum 240
ad se congregat, contra te, per nativitatem suam.

Virtutes:
O Deus, quis es tu, qui in temetipso
hoc magnum consilium habuisti,
quod destruxit infernalem haustum
in publicanis et peccatoribus, 245
qui nunc lucent in superna bonitate!
Unde, o rex, laus sit tibi.
O pater omnipotens, ex te fluit fons in igneo amore:
perduc filios tuos in rectum ventum velorum aquarum,
ita ut et nos eos hoc modo perducamus 250
in celestem Ierusalem.

238-41 The syntax of the first two verses of Chastity's speech (238-9) is somewhat awkward. This seems to reflect her rather weak response, at least initially, to the Devil's powerful attack on her status as a virtue. Indeed, Chastity's unargued retort ("your ideas are polluted and corrupt") is simply insulting. She then recovers, however, and returns to her earlier line of reasoning (229-34) that it was her particular quality that made Mary suitably pure and holy to bring forth the savior of the world. This idea would have been considered somewhat surprising by H.'s contemporaries, since salvation was for most Christians viewed more in the light of Jesus' sacrificial death on the cross than by his birth. Chastity's gynocentric perspective also contains an underlying justification for those women who choose to remain celibate in the contemporary world: since she was responsible a long time ago for the greatest good the world has ever known, women who elect today to remain chaste are in a sense making themselves latter-day Marys – perfect holy bodies that can only be spiritually consummated with their (spiritual) groom, Christ (cf. vv. 75, 104-9 and notes *ad loc.*), for the betterment of all Christians (cf. especially the words spoken by the Virtues at the beginning of the play in vv. 4-5 and notes *ad loc.* describing their "union" with Christ and its purpose: *ideo fulgemus cum illo, / edificantes membra sui pulcri corporis.*). Thus H. concludes Chastity's speech with what was the most important theme not only in this particular play but also in her life, viz., that since nuns are brides of Christ, and since the Church is the Bride of Christ, religious women have a special claim to articulate God's word in the world.

238 posset me hoc tangere = *hoc posset tangere me.* **hoc:** "this thing <which you have said>."

239 immundiciam = CL *immunditiam* < *immunditia, -ae*: "filth." **Incestus** < *incestus, -us*: "indecency," "incest."

240 protuli < *profero, -ferre.*

240-1 Cf. *John* 12.32: *et ego si exaltatus fuero a terra omnia traham ad me ipsum.* ("And I, if I am lifted up from the earth, will draw all things to myself.").

242 temetipso: an emphatic form of *te ipso.*

244 haustum: "drink"; a metaphorical image for the poison that the Devil uses to pollute people's souls.

245 publicanis: "tax collectors"; Jesus often hung out with tax collectors and "sinners"; cf., e.g., *Mark* 2.15: *et scribae et Pharisaei videntes quia manducaret cum peccatoribus et publicanis* ("And the scribes and Pharisees, seeing that he was eating with tax-collectors and sinners..."). However, the word *publicanus* in ML also meant a man who owned and ran an inn where alcohol was served. So the phrase "infernal drink" might also allude to the dangers of alcoholism.

246 superna: cf. v. 110.

248 fons in igneo: note the antithesis. H. here transforms the image of the "scorching fountain" in which the wolf was swallowed up (144-5, 220-1) into a fountain that flows from God in fiery love.

249 rectum (adj.) < *rectus, -a, -um*: "fair," "virtuous," "straight." **velorum aquarum:** "of the sails of the waters," i.e., "as they sail the seas."

251 celestem Ierusalem: cf. v. 134.

CONCLUSION

Virtutes et Anime:
In principio omnes creature viruerunt,
In medio flores floruerunt;
Postea viriditas descendit.
Et istud vir preliator vidit et dixit: 255
Hoc scio, sed aureus numerus nondum est plenus.
Tu ergo, paternum speculum aspice:
In corpore meo fatigationem sustineo,
Parvuli etiam mei deficiunt.
Nunc memor esto, quod plenitudo que in primo facta est 260
Arescere non debuit.

CONCLUSION (252-69)

The play ends with the Virtues and Anima singing in unison for the first time. Their speech begins, appropriately, with an allusion to *Genesis* 1.1. as they recall how life was in paradise (252-3) before "greenness sank away" (254; H.'s metaphor for the Fall of Man). After Christ is evoked by Anima and the Virtues as "champion," he appears to them in a vision in which he bares his wounds to God his father as he prays for the church (255-66). Interwoven into this message of human salvation are words employed earlier in the play (*speculum*, *arescere*, *oculus*, *corpus*, *vulnera*, *membra*) that recall several of the drama's themes (e.g., the mirror of life, the heavenly Jerusalem). The Virtues conclude with a final appeal to the audience to give themselves over to God/Christ so that he may reach out his hand to them (267-9).

251a Anime* = CL *Animae*.

252 in principio: cf. *Genesis* 1.1: *in principio creavit Deus caelum et terram*. **creature** = LL *creaturae* < *creatura*, *-ae*: "creation," "a created thing." **viruerunt** < *vireo*, *-ere*: "to be green," "be vigorous," "flourish."

254 viriditas: "greenness," "greening." Perhaps H.'s most important concept in her theological (and metaphorical) world-view. Baird & Ehrman (1994, 30 n. 9) state that, "*viriditas* is the very essence of life, and larger than life in Hildegard's view of the universe. It might perhaps best be rendered as "life-force"." They (1994, 7) also state that, "*viriditas* is a profound, immense, dynamically energized term. The world in the height of the spring season is filled with *viriditas*, God breathed *viriditas* into the inhabitants of the garden of Eden, even the smallest twig on the most unimportant tree is animated with *viriditas*." For more on H.'s concept of *viriditas*, see Dronke 1984, 82-7.

255 preliator = CL *proeliator* < *proeliator*, *-oris*: "champion," "combatant"; the *preliator* is Christ.

256 hoc: the pronoun probably refers to the idea *viriditas descendit* in v. 254. **aureus numerus:** apparently referring to the number of souls who will be saved.

257 paternum speculum: H. reworks the phrase "mirror of life" encountered in v. 93 into that of a "paternal mirror." The syntax is elliptical and the metaphor somewhat bizarre, but after interpreting 258-66 and reading backwards, its meaning seems to be the following: Christ is asking God to look at his own (i.e., Christ's) body as God's "mirror." It seems, therefore, that in this verse and the following one Christ is both recalling to his father his own redemptive suffering on behalf of mankind and simultaneously interceding for humans with God once again in the present (cf. 265-6 and notes *ad loc.*).

258 sustineo < *sustineo*, *-ere*: "to suffer," "endure."

259 deficiunt < *deficio*, *-ire*: "to grow weak," "faint."

260 in primo: synonymous with *in principio*.

261 arescere: cf. v. 111. **Non debuit:** "need not."

Et tunc in te habuisti
Quod oculus tuus numquam cederet
Usque dum corpus meum videres plenum gemmarum.
Nam me fatigat quod omnia membra mea in irrisionem vadunt. 265
Pater, vide, vulnera mea tibi ostendo.
Ergo nunc, omnes homines,
Genua vestra ad patrem vestrum flectite,
Ut vobis manum suam porrigat.

262 in te habuisti: i.e., "you resolved."

264 usque dum: "until." **corpus . . . plenum gemmarum:** a compressed metaphorical image of the wounded Christ's bleeding body. The phrase *plenum gemmarum* can also mean "full of buds," thus viewing Christ's body as the tree of life in full bloom. This phrase also recalls the image of the heavenly Jerusalem, a city "full of gems" (cf. *Apocalypse* 21, a chapter devoted to a description of the celestial Jerusalem; especially relevant are v. 11 "[holy Jerusalem] having the glory of God, its radiance like a most rare jewel, like a jasper, clear as crystal" and v. 19 "The foundations of the wall of the city were adorned with every jewel."). H.'s medical writings include discussions of the powerful healing properties of certain gems.

265 irrisionem < *irrisio, -onis*: "ridicule," "mockery." The meaning of this verse is twofold. Christ is both reliving his experience on the cross and metaphorically describing the mockery of the Church (*omnia membra mea*; cf. v. 5 and note *ad loc.*).

269 porrigat: cf. v. 138.

Appendix A

The Feast of Fools

The Feast of Fools is a catchall phrase that embraces various winter festivals held during the Christmas season in Western Europe from the 5th-16th centuries. The most famous of these was held on Jan. 1, and involved a reversal of the status of the church hierarchy as inferior clergy (subdeacons) assumed the roles of their superiors. Another feast closely related to the Feast of Fools was the Feast of the Ass, held on Jan. 14, in which an ass was led into the church from the street (to the accompaniment of the shout "giddy-up"; see v. 225 of the *Danielis Ludus* and note *ad loc.*) and celebrated for his unsung roles in the life of Jesus. (The ass was present at his birth and also bore him through Jerusalem on Palm Sunday.) The *Danielis Ludus* seems to have incorporated elements of both of these feasts, and may actually be a central component of the Feast of Fools as it was celebrated in Beauvais.

Fassler (1990) has argued that the *Danielis Ludus* was part of the reform movement by the priests and bishop of Beauvais to control the outlandish and often sacrilegious behavior of the secular clergy and minor orders. This seems to explain certain aspects (some of them unusual) about the play: the occasional use of raucous music and dance; Darius' comical shout of *O hez*! (225); the choice of subject (youthful hero makes good) and theme (impiety and blasphemy punished). Thus one other function of this multifaceted work may have been to rechannel the youthful energies of the students and scholars of Beauvais into what the religious authorities believed was a much more appropriate expression of their role (as reflected by and through the church) in society.

Harris (2011), in an important new book, both modifies and pushes Fassler's interpretation further, and attempts to show that the Feast of Fools developed in the late twelfth and early thirteenth centuries as an elaborate and orderly liturgy for Feast of the Circumcision of Christ (1 January) – serving as a dignified alternative to rowdy secular New Year festivities. The intent of the feast, Harris believes, was not mockery but thanksgiving for the incarnation of Christ (cf. the very first words of the *Danielis Ludus*: *Ad honorem tui, Christe*).

Appendix B

Danielis Ludus – Discography

Listed below are the audio recordings of the *Danielis Ludus* currently available (as of July 2013) as CDs and/or MP3 downloads.

1. *The Play of Daniel / The Play of Herod*
   Conductor: Noah Greenberg
   Orchestra: New York Pro Musica
   Label: MCA Classics
   Date: January 1, 1995 (originally recorded in 1958)

2. *Ludus Danielis*
   Conductor: Janka Szendrei
   Orchestra: Schola Hungarica
   Label: Hungaroton/White Label (Hun)
   Date: October 18, 1994 (originally recorded in 1984)

3. *ludus danielis*
   Conductor: Michael Popp
   Orchestra: Estampie
   Label: Christophorus (German)
   Date: January 19, 1997

4. *Ludus Danielis-Play of Daniel*
   Conductor: Andrew Lawrence-King
   Orchestra: Harp Consort
   Label: Bmg/Deutsche Harmonia Mundi
   Date: November 10, 1998

5. *Daniel and the Lions*
   Conductor: Frederick Renz
   Orchestra: New York Ensemble for Early Music
   Label: Fone (Italy)
   Date: January 29, 1999

6. *Ludus Danielis*
   Conductor: Renee Clemencic
   Orchestra: Clemencic Consort
   Label: Aura Classics
   Date: December 28, 1999

7. *The Play of Daniel*
   Conductor: William Lyons
   Orchestra: The Dufay Collective
   Label: Harmonia Mundi U.S.A.
   Date: August 12, 2008

Appendix C

Four Letters of Hildegard

H. was a voluminous letter writer, and her correspondence with an emperor, a pope, bishops, abbots, abbesses, priors, monks and nuns often illuminates various aspects of her life and her work. The four letters printed below come from different periods of her life but all deal with themes and ideas that are prominent in the *Ordo Virtutum*. The first three letters, translated by Joseph L. Baird and Radd K. Ehrman are taken from their first volume of H.'s correspondence (Baird & Ehrman 1994, 128-30, 136, and 195-6, respectively) and appear courtesy of Oxford University Press. The fourth letter, not yet catalogued, is translated by Peter Dronke (in Dronke 1984, 184) and appears courtesy of Cambridge University Press.

A. 52r: Hildegard to the Congregation of Nuns (1148-50)

[This letter is in response to one sent to H. by a certain Tengswich, a superior of a foundation of canonnesses, who (rather ironically) inquired into H.'s unusual practices concerning H.'s nuns with respect to their attire, behavior, and the fact that they all come from the aristocracy (Tengswich had noted in her letter that Jesus himself had recruited his disciples from the poor).]

The Living Fountain says: Let a woman remain within her chamber so that she may preserve her modesty, for the serpent breathed the fiery danger of horrible lust into her. Why should she do this? Because the beauty of woman radiated and blazed forth in the primordial root, and in her was formed that chamber in which every creature lies hidden. Why is she so resplendent? For two reasons: on the one hand, because she was created by the finger of God and, on the other, because she was endowed with wondrous beauty. O, woman, what a splendid being you are! For you have set your foundation in the sun, and have conquered the world.

Paul the apostle, who flew to the heights but kept silent on earth so as not to reveal that which was hidden [cf. II Cor 12.2ff.], observed that a woman who is subject to the power of her husband [cf. Ephes 5.22 ff; Col 3.18], joined to him through the first rib, ought to preserve great modesty, by no means giving or displaying her vessel to another man who has no business with her, for that vessel belongs to her husband [cf. I Thess 4.4]. And let her do this in accordance with the word spoken by the master of the earth ill scorn of the devil: "What God hath joined together, let no man put asunder" [Matt 19.6].

Listen: The earth keeps the grass green and vital, until winter conquers it. Then winter takes away the beauty of that flower, and the earth covers over its vital force so that it is unable to manifest itself as if it had never withered up, because winter has ravaged it. In a similar manner, a woman, once married, ought not to indulge herself in prideful adornment of hair or person, nor ought she to lift herself up to vanity, wearing a crown and other golden ornaments, except at her husband's pleasure, and even then with moderation.

But these strictures do not apply to a virgin, for she stands in the unsullied purity of paradise, lovely and unwithering, and she always remains in the full vitality of the budding rod. A virgin is not commanded to cover up her hair, but she willingly does so out of her great humility, for a person will naturally hide the beauty of her soul, lest, on account of her pride, the hawk carry it off. Virgins are married with holiness in the Holy Spirit and in the bright dawn of virginity, and so it is proper that they come before the great High Priest as an oblation presented to God. Thus through the permission granted her and the revelation of the mystic inspiration of the finger of God, it is appropriate for a virgin to wear a white vestment, the lucent symbol of her betrothal to Christ, considering that her mind is made one "with the interwoven whole, and keeping in mind the One to whom she is joined, as it is written: "Having his name, and the name of his Father, written on their foreheads" [Apoc 14.1] and also "These follow the Lamb whithersoever he goeth" [Apoc 14.4].

God also keeps a watchful eye on every person, so that a lower order will not gain ascendancy over a higher one, as Satan and the first man did, who wanted to fly higher than they had been placed. And who would gather all his livestock indiscriminately into one barn—the cattle, the asses, the sheep, the kids? Thus it is clear that differentiation must be maintained in these matters, lest people of varying status, herded all together, be dispersed through the pride of their elevation, on the one hand, or the disgrace of their decline, on the other, and especially lest the nobility of their character be torn asunder when they slaughter one another out of hatred. Such destruction naturally results when the higher order falls upon the lower, and the lower rises above the higher. For God establishes ranks on earth, just as in heaven with angels, archangels, thrones, dominions, cherubim, and seraphim. And they are all loved by God, although they are not equal in rank. Pride loves princes and nobles because of their illusions of grandeur, but hates them when they destroy that illusion. And it is written that "God does not cast off the mighty since He himself is mighty" [Job 36.5]. He does not love people for their rank but for their works which derive their savor from Him, just as the Son of God says: "My food is to do the will of my Father" [John 4.34]. Where humility is found, there Christ always prepares a banquet. Thus when individuals seek after empty honor rather than humility, because they believe that one is preferable to the other, it is necessary that they be assigned to their proper place. Let the sick sheep be cast out of the fold, lest it infect the entire flock.

God has infused human beings with good understanding so that their name will not be destroyed. It is not good for people to grab hold of a mountain which they cannot possibly move. Rather, they should stand in the valley, gradually learning what they are capable of.

These words do not come from a human being but from the Living Light. Let the one who hears see and believe where these words come from.

B. 58: Hildegard to Prior Dimo (1169-70)

[A general admonition couched in allegorical terms.]

I saw and heard these words in a true vision: Life sees death and overcomes it, just as David, a little boy, conquered Goliath. A mountain is visible because it is lofty, and a valley lies beneath it, sometimes causing flowers to bud in their vitality, but more often producing useless weeds, nettles, and thorns.

Now, understand, O man. Two men were sitting in a house, one of whom was a knight; the other, a serf. And two wise and beautiful girls came to that house, knocked on the door, and said to them: You have become notorious even in far distant lands, for many people allege that you have slandered the king, and the king has asked, Who are these miscreants to be saying such things about me? Therefore, you two, hear our advice, for it will bring you victory. I am Humility: I have seen life in the incarnation of the Son of God, and I have crushed Death under my heel. The works of obedience are a mountain, and benevolence is a valley lush with flowers, though frequently choked off by nettles and thorns watered by the storms of sins.

Listen, therefore, O man, for it is the house of your heart that the knight and the serf – that is, Obedience and Pride are sitting in, and it is at the door of your mind that the two girls – that is, Divine Love and Humility – are knocking, to prevent you from committing all the sins that you are capable of. Now, therefore, observe that the knight defeats the serf, lest he trample the beauty of obedience beneath his feet, for Pride says, Those chains with which I bind mankind cannot be broken. But respond to him in the words of Love: I sat unsullied in heaven, and I kissed the earth. Pride swore against me and wanted to fly higher than the stars, but I threw him into the abyss. Now, therefore, join me in trampling the serf underfoot, my son, and take your stand with me, Divine Love, and embrace Humility as your lady. Thus you will escape condemnation and eternal death.

C. 85r/b: Hildegard to Adam, the Abbot (before 1166)

[In a previous letter to Adam, H. presented an allegorical discourse on divine love and creation. In this second letter to the abbot H. continues her advice to him in the form of another elaborate allegory.]

He Who Is says: The sun shines and sends forth its rays. And a certain man, a friend of the sun, had a garden in which he desired to plant many herbs and flowers. And the sun, in the fire of its rays, sent heat upon those herbs and flowers, and the dew and rain gave the moisture of viridity to them. Then from the north a contorted figure with black hair and horrible face came to that garden, but at the same time from the east came a handsome young man with bright shining hair and a comely, pleasant face. And the contorted figure said to the young man: Where have you come from? And he answered: I come from the east to the garden of this wise man, for I greatly desired to come to him. And the contorted figure said: Listen to me: A destructive wind and hail and fire and pestilence will come upon that garden, and will dry it out. But the young man answered: Not so, it will not be so, because I do not wish it, and I will bring forth a pure fountain and will irrigate the garden. And the contorted figure answered: Ha! That is as possible as if locusts would eat through hard rock. And so that crafty figure brought winter into that garden and sought to dry up the herbs and flowers. And that aforementioned young man, caught up in playing his harp did not see what was happening. But when he did take notice, he called the sun back with a loud sound, and the sun came into Taurus and brought the viridity of summer back into that garden. And taking up an ivory horn and a hart horn, with them he cast that contorted figure down to the earth. And then he said to the man who owned the garden: From now on, do not rely so fully on yourself that you fail to enclose your garden with a high wall, so that the black birds in the storms will not be able to dry it up.

Now, you, O Father, understand these words spoken to you, for you have the highest of all callings as Christ's representative. Listen, therefore: The grace of God shines like the sun and sends its gifts in various ways: in wisdom, in viridity, in moisture. But wisdom can degenerate into grossness, viridity can fall under great labor, and moisture can turn into harsh bitterness. But you, O friend of the grace of God, you have a garden of people, in which as the representative of Christ you seek to plant many wholesome desires and good works. And through the power of His gifts, the grace of God pours out His dynamic good will upon those desires and those works, and causes the garden to grow green through the dew and the rain of the fountain of living water [see Cant 4.15, Jer 2.13; cf. John 4.11, 7.38].

But vices come from the devil in the turmoil of vainglory and the uproar of impertinence which fights against just governance, but the virtues, planted by God, burgeon in divine love with the full benevolence of proper discipline and complete contempt for the world, springing up for the benefit of the people. And the vices ask the virtues why they have come. And they answer that they have come from God to the people of the friend of God, because they greatly desire to build a sacrifice of praise in them. And the vices respond: Great ruin and ire and insidious interrogations that cause great distress will fall upon this people, so that they will grow weary in their service to God. And the virtues respond: That will not happen, because we will not cease from doing good, but the fountain of living water will pour forth and will defend this people with its compassion. But, with scornful laughter, the devil's vices say that this is as possible as if fragile flesh were to remain unblemished and unwrinkled. Then the crafty vices bring the cold cloud of ignorance upon this people, so that their wholesome desires and their good works fail, because they have faith in themselves alone. But showing obedience in their praises to God, the virtues permit this thing to be done by the just judgment of God, so that men may understand what they are. And so when the people come to their senses in humility, the virtues zealously tender the grace of God to them in order to impress the passion of Christ on their minds, so that the people may be brought back to their pristine praise of God. Thus by looking to the divinity and humanity of the Son of God, they cast those vices down to contrition. And to the leader of those people, they say: Warned by these things, do not trust in your powers alone, but see to it that you flee to the grace of God, so that you may protect and admonish your people in every way, lest the treacheries of the devil turn them aside into all sorts of vices through negligence.

And you also, O father, hear us: As the morning star comes before the dawn, offer your help to us with the kiss of love which God gave to you. And God will give you that life which He looked upon on the first day.

D. Hildegard to an Unknown Addressee (date unknown)

"The mountains ascend and the fields descend to the place you have established for them." That is: the ascent of the mountain means God's might, and the descent of the field means his potential; and in these two parts he places and divides all things, for he has set the heaven into the height, and his own light – that is, the earth – beneath him, and has ordained this placing in the whole of creation. Pride contradicted this, and claimed the likeness of equality with God, which cannot be; so it was accounted as naught by him – for if a man were without his wings of arms and hands, the human form which is in him would be accounted as naught. The godhead prepared heaven and all its hidden places, and built up all creatures in their lands, and the earth sustains them. But Pride's effort at building lacks both head and wings, and Pride can scarcely stand even on one foot, and cannot walk.

That it lacks head and wings means it is without God; nor has it any possibility of standing upright, but always falls, and sets up each of its works mendaciously, in nothing but a word. Without the body of truth, it is trying to stand on one foot – which means a lie – but he who has two feet cannot walk on one. So let all the faithful flee from Pride, which always consists in lying, for it cannot be called craftsman either in bronze or earthenware. So it builds nothing, either in heavenly or earthly things, but is the destroyer and despoiler of what is built – for it lost heaven and deceived man, as Scripture tells.

Appendix D

Hildegard of Bingen: Sound & Vision

Listed below are the two audio recordings currently available (as of July 2013) of Hildegard's *Ordo Virtutum* and the sole video performance of it released commercially.

A. Compact Discs/MP3 Downloads

1. *Hildegard von Bingen: Ordo Virtutum*
   Performers: Sequentia
   Label: Bmg/Deutsche Harmonia Mundi
   Catalogue #77394
   Date: April 7, 1998

[A two-disc performance of H.'s play, with interpolated instrumental music. What this performance lacks in dramatic intensity it more than makes up for in purity and beauty of sound. The entire 90-minute performance has been uploaded by Sequentia to YouTube: http://www.youtube.com/watch?v=O2aKyH2NhW0]

2. *Hildegard von Bingen: Ordo Virtutum*
   Performers: Vox Animae
   Label: Etcetera (Netherlands)
   Catalogue #1203
   Date: January 18, 2005 (originally recorded in 1997)

[A slightly earthier, less polished performance of H.'s music drama than Sequentia's recording. Vox Animae interprets the work from a more theatrical perspective. Their tempos are quicker than the Sequentia version, and there is less interpolated instrumental music.]

B. Video

1. *Hildegard Von Bingen In Portrait: Ordo Virtutum*
   Director: Michael Fields
   Performers: Vox Animae
   Studio: KULTUR VIDEO
   Format: DVD
   Date: 2008

[This is the same musical performance of Vox Animae as the one used in their audio production (see A above). The performance is also available on YouTube: http://www.youtube.com/watch?v=q4x46bBawUo]

Bibliography

Avalle 1984. Avalle, d'A. S. *Il teatro medievale e il Ludus Danielis*. Turin, 1984.

Avalle 1987. Avalle, d'A. S. '*Secundum speculationem rationemve* (Il "Ludus Danielis" di Beauvais)', *Helikon* XXII-XXVII (1982-1987) 3-59.

Baird & Ehrman 1994. Baird, Joseph L. and Radd K. Ehrman (edd.). *The Letters of Hildegard of Bingen*. Vol. I. New York, 1994.

Bevington 1975. Bevington, David. *Medieval Drama*. Boston, 1975.

Browne 1959. Browne, E. Martin. "Preface." In *Play of Daniel, a Thirteenth Century Musical Drama*, ed. by Noah Greenberg (New York, 1959) v-vi.

Cantor 1993. Cantor, Norman F. *The Civilization of the Middle Ages*. New York, 1993.

Chambers, 1903. Chambers, E. K. *The Medieval Stage*. Oxford, 1903. (Reprinted by Dover Publications, Inc., New York, 1996).

Collins 1996. Collins, Fletcher. "*The Play of Daniel* in Modern Performances." In *The Play of Daniel: Critical Essays* (Early Drama, Art, and Music Monograph Series, 24), ed. Dunbar H. Ogden (Kalamazoo, 1996) 63-75.

Davidson 1992. Davidson, Audrey Ekdahl. "Music and Performance: Hildegard of Bingen's *Ordo Virtutum*." In *The* Ordo Virtutum *of Hildegard of Bingen: Critical Studies* (Early Drama, Art, and Music Monograph Series, 18), ed. Audrey Ekdahl Davidson (Kalamazoo, 1992)1-29.

Davidson 1996. Davidson, Audrey Ekdahl. "Music in the Beauvais *Ludus Danielis*." In *The Play of Daniel: Critical Essays* (Early Drama, Art, and Music Monograph Series, 24), ed. Dunbar H. Ogden (Kalamazoo, 1996) 77-86.

Dentan 1993. Dentan, Robert C. "Bel and the Dragon." In *The Oxford Companion to the Bible*, edd. Bruce M. Metzger and Michael D. Coogan (Oxford, 1993) 77.

Dronke 1970. Dronke, Peter. *Poetic Individuality in the Middle Ages. New Departures in Poetry 1000-1150*. London, 1970.

Dronke 1984. Dronke, Peter. *Women Writers of the Middle Ages*. Cambridge, 1984.

Dronke 1985. Dronke, Peter. "Symphoniae." In *Hildegard von Bingen*: *Symphonia* (audio recording), performed by Sequentia (Deutsche Harmonia Mundi 77020-2-RG) 8-9.

Dronke 1994. Dronke, Peter. *Nine Medieval Latin Plays* (Cambridge Medieval Classics, No. 1). Cambridge, 1994.

Emmerson 1996. Emmerson, Richard K. "Divine Judgment and Local Ideology in the Beauvais *Ludus Danielis*." In *The Play of Daniel: Critical Essays* (Early Drama, Art, and Music Monograph Series, 24), ed. Dunbar H. Ogden (Kalamazoo, 1996) 33-61.

Fassler 1991. Fassler, Margot. "Representations of Time in *Ordo representacionis Ade*." In *Contexts: Style and Values in Medieval Art and Literature*, ed. Daniel Poirion and Nancy Freeman Regalado, *Yale French Studies*, special issue (1991) 97-113.

Fassler 1992. Fassler, Margot. "The Feast of Fools and *Danielis Ludus*: Popular Tradition in a Medieval Cathedral Play." In *Plainsong in the Age of Polyphony*, ed. Thomas Forrest Kelly (Cambridge, 1992) 65-99.

Flanagan 1989. Flanagan, Sabina. *Hildegard of Bingen: A Visionary Life*. New York, 1989.

Greenberg 1959. Greenberg, Noah (ed.). *Play of Daniel, a Thirteenth Century Musical Drama*. New York, 1959.

Harrington & Pucci 1997. Harrington, K. P. (revised by Joseph Pucci). *Medieval Latin*[2]. Chicago, 1997.

Harris 1992. Harris, John Wesley. Medieval Theatre in Context: An Introduction. London, 1992.

Harris 2011. Harris, Max. *Sacred Folly: A New History of the Feast of Fools*. Ithaca, N.Y., 2011.

Hollister 1982. Hollister, C. Warren. *Medieval Europe: A Short History*[5]. New York, 1982.

Iversen 1992. Iversen, Gunilla. "*Ego Humilitatis, regina Virtutum*: Poetic Language and Literary Structure in Hildegard of Bingen's Vision of the Virtues." In *The* Ordo Virtutum *of Hildegard of Bingen: Critical Studies* (Early Drama, Art, and Music Monograph Series, 18), ed. Audrey Ekdahl Davidson (Kalamazoo, 1992) 79-110.

Iversen 1997. Iversen, Gunilla. "O Virginitas, in regali thalmo stas; New Light on the *Ordo Virtutum*: Hildegard, Richardis, and the Order of the Virtues," *EDAMR* 20, no. 1 (Fall 1997) 1-16.

Muir 1995. Muir, Lynette R. The Biblical Drama of Medieval Europe. Cambridge, 1995.

Newman, 1987. Newman, Barbara. *Sister of Wisdom*: *St. Hildegard's Theology of the Feminine*. Berkeley, 1987.

Ogden 1996a. Ogden, Dunbar H. "Introduction." In *The Play of Daniel: Critical Essays* (Early Drama, Art, and Music Monograph Series, 24), ed. Dunbar H. Ogden (Kalamazoo, 1997) 1-9.

Ogden 1996b. Ogden, Dunbar H. "The Staging of The Play of Daniel in the Twelfth Century." In *The Play of Daniel: Critical Essays* (Early Drama, Art, and Music Monograph Series, 24), ed. Dunbar H. Ogden (Kalamazoo, 1997) 11-32.

Paterno 1989. Paterno, Salvatore. The Liturgical Context of Early European Drama. Potomac (Maryland), 1989.

Pinsky 1998. Pinsky, Robert. *The Sounds of Poetry*. New York, 1998.

Potter 1992. Potter, Robert. "The *Ordo Virtutum*: Ancestor of the English Moralities?" In *The* Ordo Virtutum *of Hildegard of Bingen: Critical Studies* (Early Drama, Art, and Music Monograph Series, 18), ed. Audrey Ekdahl Davidson (Kalamazoo, 1992) 31-41.

Stevens 1980. Stevens, John. 'Medieval Drama.' In *The New Grove Dictionary of Music and Musicians*, ed. Stanley Sadie (London, 1980), XII, 36-7.

Sticca 1985. Sticca, Sandro. 'Sacred Drama and Tragic Realism in Hrotswitha's *Paphnutius*.' In *The Theatre in the Middle Ages*, edd. Herman Braet, Johan Nowe, Gilbert Tournoy (Leuven, 1985) 12-44.

Wulstan 1976. Wulstan, David. "Introduction." In *The Play of Daniel: A Mediaeval Liturgical Drama*, ed. W. L. Smoldon, revised by David Wulstan (Sutton, 1976) i-vi.

Made in the USA
Coppell, TX
24 January 2023

11660802R00085